Also by Don C. Nix

Loss of Being

The Field of Being

Moments of Grace

Patterns of Being

Dancing with Presence

The Crucible of the Miraculous

The Matrix of Splendor

The Rainbow Earth

The Ocean of Livingness

First Light

This Shimmering Life

The Sea of Sensitivity

*Collected Thoughts on
Consciousness and Reality*

by Don C. Nix, J.D., Ph.D.

iUniverse, Inc.
Bloomington

The Sea of Sensitivity

iUniverse books may be ordered through booksellers or by contacting:

iUniverse
1663 Liberty Drive
Bloomington, IN 47403
www.iuniverse.com
1-800-Authors (1-800-288-4677)

ISBN: 978-1-4620-6168-6 (sc)
ISBN: 978-1-4620-6169-3 (e)

Printed in the United States of America

iUniverse rev. date: 10/20/2011

Dedication

To Rick Tarnas, for his determination, hard work, his dedication to Truth and his courage in speaking it, even when it flies in the face of the opinions of the cultural complex. You and others like you are the way that we will evolve ourselves into an emerging, unknown and surprising future.

Contents

Introduction

Wonder is the invisible component of transformation. It is a special kind of consciousness, an expanded state that involves both the mind and the heart. It focuses the mind on generative Being, and produces a subtle thrill throughout the mind and body, as perceptions of and connection to the Cosmos emerge in experience. Wonder opens the mind to Being, and the body to experiences of depth and sacredness. If the state persists for any length of time, it will create experiences of mystery and infinity. It opens the eyes. It opens the heart. It generates gratitude, as we contemplate the grace cascading upon us, and perceive ourselves in a context of Vastness. It causes us, for a moment, to step outside of our separateness and open ourselves to the Cosmos.

Wonder is vastly under-rated. It is not usually considered in the list of human experiences that we consider to be important states in life, such as love, compassion and joy. It deserves more of our attention, however, because wonder is a unique door opening, a portal to connection with the invisible, living, generative Field of Being that surrounds us and sustains our life on this Earth. Wonder is, in the moment, a heightened sensitivity to the miraculous that enfolds us every moment that we are alive. It lifts us out of our torpor. If we can wake ourselves from our sleep, we will find ourselves living in a perpetual state of wonder.

1
A Handful of Diamonds

I wake from darkness.
My mind lights up.
A handful of tiny diamonds,
radiant and reflective,
faceted and self-luminous,
sending and receiving,
in a pool of Living Light.
I rest in Its sensitive brilliance
and connect to the Cosmos.
Another day on Earth.

We live in a vast Sea of Sensitivity. We call it the Cosmos. It is an ocean of invisible Livingness that, when we turn to look at it, is astounding. This infinite pool of pure awareness cannot be seen with the eyes, but we can directly experience it with the cells of our bodies. The Sea generates everything in the material realm that we see around us. That part of the Sea that we are allowed to directly access we call our consciousness.

The Sea is omnipresent in our lives. It connects us to our world. It makes it possible to be alive. It is pure Livingness, pure Being, that has graced us by sharing Itself with us for a period of time. It is our greatest gift.

We rarely notice the pool of Living Space behind our eyes. Like fish swimming in the ocean, we are unaware of our basic medium. We can be forgiven for overlooking this, our primary miracle. It is wholly intangible. We can perceive Its effects, but it has no substance for our perceptions to hook into. Living space is dynamic. It makes things happen. Reality emerges out of It. It is generative. It continually throws forth and metamorphoses the universe, deleting the worn-out from existence and ushering in the fresh and the new. It is continually throwing up structures never before seen in the universe. We call that creativity.

It is our link to life, endowed by living Mystery to enable us to participate in reality, both inner and outer. It is an exquisite sensitivity to the creation of the Cosmos. It enables us to perceive reality, orient ourselves in time and space, and proceed with the business of living.

Another reason that we do not often perceive the pool is that it is covered by thoughts. The pool is not the same as thoughts. Thoughts are momentary confluences of energy that appear, move through the pool of consciousness and disappear, to be succeeded by the next. We live each day with our thoughts strung like pearls on a string, one after the other, moving though consciousness. The pool itself, the living Field that hosts the thoughts, lies serenely and silently beneath them. It is the medium that they float through, the invisible, alive Field that holds and records them as they traverse our minds.

The moving thoughts seize all of our attention. In our restless jousting with Reality, we are aware primarily of our thoughts as we plot and plan our strategies to try to keep ourselves safe and flourish in the world. We become mesmerized by the siren of our thoughts and their relations to the turbulent world. As tiny children, we begin an internal conversation with ourselves that lasts a lifetime. That conversation is so compelling that it demands and receives our full attention over a lifetime. In the process, we overlook the silent, underlying, alive, impressionable Field that makes the conversation possible.

The Field of awareness within the human being is pure Being. It is the primary component of reality, both at the interior, personal level and at the cosmic level of the Universe. It is alive, conscious, intelligent and infinitely mysterious, a Field of Sensitivity and life that is the Matrix of all of our experience.

Our individual consciousness is that part of Being to which we are given temporary access. It is on loan to us. In due time, it will be taken back. While we have it, however, it supports our life, registers our experience, and allows our personal sound and light show to continue.

The experience of consciousness is like having a handful of diamonds in our head. These are no ordinary diamonds. Like their carbon counterparts in the material world, they catch light in their facets and send it in many directions. Unlike carbon diamonds, they are living and self-luminous, lit from within by the very fires of Life itself. Our experience of our consciousness is an experience of being lit up inside our head. We are bathed in light internally as we watch from some mysterious vantage point the phantom images that parade through our minds.

Another way of thinking about this is to focus on subatomic particles, the material equivalents of the diamonds of consciousness. The subatomic particles in our brains are very talented. We know that our material brains are composed, like all matter, of electrons circling around their nuclei. At these microcosmic levels, we are mostly space—intelligent space—with a few floating packets of energy and information widely separated from each other. This is the nature of all material, including our brain. Scientists have no idea how the leap occurs from the material brain to totally immaterial consciousness. They have concluded that the material brain somehow produces the miracle of consciousness. Having leapt over this crucial chasm, they have proceeded to map the brain to determine which portion of it fires to produce each phenomena of conscious experience. Beneath this entire enterprise is the dying assumption that assumes that the material realm is the only true reality. The scientists, in looking for the way that the material brain produces non-material awareness, are asking the wrong question. The assumption that matter produces consciousness has it backward. The prime reality in the universe is consciousness, innate and fundamental to Being throughout the universe. The material realm emerges as a byproduct of this invisible Livingness. We do not invent ourselves or our awareness. We are not the result of haphazard accident involving material molecules. We emerge from universal Life, the intentional recipients of life, experience and consciousness.

Living, generative space is not only the nature of our experience inside our head. It is also the nature of the entire Cosmos. The material level of reality is secondary to it, an effect of its cause. Being, in all of its invisible mystery, is the generative source of both consciousness and material. Perhaps we have only now matured to the point where we can begin to see this. We are still evolving out of our primitive animal past. We are still encountering new realities as our evolution proceeds. Contemplating the mystery of consciousness is still a stretch for us. We must, and will, grow in time into a larger awareness that puts Being and Living Consciousness at the center of our understanding of reality.

2
The Primate Mind

Deep in my cells,
I remember...
swimming with scales and gills,
the fire in the cave,
making pictures for the hunt,
and the miracle of discovering grains,
creating cities of stone,
the wars of my Liege-Lord,
and cloisters under silent towers,
discovering the luminous Self,
when my mind awoke,
to daylight and vastness and time.

We live out our lives in an ocean of mystery. We are born. We grow. But, by the time that we are becoming aware of our environment at two or three, it has already been stripped of its magic by familiarity. Our earliest encounters are with the hard world of materiality, the surface of reality. Most of us will continue throughout our lives perceiving only this obvious, superficial level, never questioning that it is the ultimate reality, although our science tells us that the solidity of the world is an illusion. Far beneath the level of our senses and perceptions floats a realm of sub-atomic particles that is mostly living space. We cannot perceive this sub-atomic reality as we go about our daily lives, but it is always there, as real as our kitchen table or the family car.

Also beneath perception and similarly overlooked is the realm of invisible, pure Being that generates and supports the material world. This deep level of reality is alive and conscious. It can never be seen, though we can see its handiwork everywhere around us, patterned and perfectly collated together by its fierce intelligence. We ourselves are continually thrown up by Being, to evolve into destinies that we cannot fathom. All this is the magical Cosmos, the enchanted world that we manage to overlook and ignore for a lifetime.

How do we manage that? How do we overlook the central core of reality? The answer must have to do with evolution. We are simply not evolved enough yet to grasp all of reality. We are still a work in progress. With our immense gifts of self-awareness, reasoning, creativity and language, we can see the results of our previous evolution, but it does not occur to us that more metamorphosis lies ahead.

We are still evolving out of the primate mind. We know that not so long ago we were searching for food in the trees. Then we came down onto the savannahs, stood up on two legs, and learned to throw things to get food. Today, we have put a man on the moon, eradicated terrible, crippling diseases, and organized a net of world communication. We are clearly evolving at an astonishing rate.

Yet, the evolution seems uneven. Our ceaseless wars and our lack of concern for our fellow man, our animal co-journers, and the planet itself spring out of that part of the primate mind that has not yet sufficiently evolved. In certain respects, we now need an evolutionary jump-start to a larger consciousness, or else we risk destroying ourselves and our world.

The primate mind is a small, localized mind, fixated on self-interest and individual, personal problems. Except in rare moments of panoramic consciousness, it revolves around immediate, self-concerned issues of food, safety and personal status. It is incessantly preoccupied with improving its lot and clawing its way to greater status. This mind is characterized by its obsession with a string of problems. As fast as one problem is solved, another takes its place. It is the problem-solving mind. It is enmeshed in its material concerns for itself, and almost never raises its head to contemplate the magnificence of the context. Most of Reality escapes it in its preoccupation with itself and its immediate problems.

The mind's primate orientation produces a sense of emptiness, desolation and alienation. It generates continual feelings of vulnerability. Fear is never far away. It perceives no ground of support for itself. Being is not available. It is not even in the framework, so support from the ground of Being is non-existent. As a result, the primate mind feels constantly threatened. It is cut off from the only source of strength and succor and holding in the universe—invisible, conscious, living Being. The primate mind perceives nothing underneath it. It is on its own, and it is far too small to be up to the task. It attempts to plow through life as best it can, and to flourish without access to its Source. No wonder it produces despair.

Through the centuries the primate mind has been identified many times and by many traditions. It has been called the ego, the personality, the constructed self, the false self, etc. These labels all refer to basically the same thing—a small, self-preoccupied consciousness so wrapped up in its own personal concerns that it lacks perception of the mysterious, shimmering magic show that is all around us. The Cosmos is waiting for us to wake up and grow up.

3
Creativity

Creativity flows through me,
not from me,
and I realize
it's not really mine.
The impulse to craft
something new and fine
is rooted in Power
so deep and profound
that a glimpse of It
stills my mind.

Creativity and consciousness are the same phenomenon. The awareness that powers our brain and also the world is not passive and inert space. It is generative, an immensely powerful, active Field that brings reality into being, whether that reality consists of images in the mind or forms in the material world. We live out our lives in a supremely, mysterious Matrix that constantly creates and metamorphoses reality. We call it Being. It is unseen and unseeable, without form Itself but generating at every moment all the forms in the world around us, including ourselves, and every image forming and moving through our minds. It is a miraculous Field of pure, incessant creativity.

From the time that we came out of the trees, humans have encountered and felt this vast, invisible Livingness around them. However, since It is entirely without form, they found it difficult to grasp, describe, hold in consciousness, and communicate It. So, all over the world humans created symbolic great gods of the sky and great gods of the earth, usually in a human semblance. Demonic, fearful, bestial figures were also created to represent powerful, dangerous forces perceived in nature. In short order, it was forgotten that these god-figures were symbols, stand-ins for the unseeable Presence in the Cosmos. The symbol figures began to be worshipped for themselves, and elaborate stories were created around them to explain the intricacies of life and man's relation to the Cosmos.

For millennia, these symbolic god-figures in many forms claimed the allegiance of humans. About 400 years ago in the West, a process of deconstructing the god-symbols began with the work of Isaac Newton and Rene Descartes. In succeeding centuries, the symbols eroded in Western consciousness. They were discredited by the incremental, successful discoveries of science, which focused itself exclusively on the material level of existence. Over time, we arrived where we are now, bereft of awareness of both god-representations in symbolic form and invisible, living Being. We became separated from the Ground of our being, leaving us empty, in desolation and despair, and desperate for some sort of meaning. This is where we find ourselves today.

The universe has responded with creative solutions to similar crises in the past. At one point, oxygen, which was a waste product of successful life-forms on earth, collected in such great quantities in the atmosphere that it threatened all life on earth. The universe found a way out. It developed prolific life-forms like blue-green algae that began to eat the oxygen out of the air. The oxygen component in the atmosphere was reduced and stabilized at 21%, where it has remained ever since. That creative solution to the problem enabled our lives and all other life on Earth to continue.

Today, it is possible that another creative solution is developing to evolve our consciousness out of its present cul-de-sac. Quantum physics has taken science into totally new territory in the last half-century. It has been proved conclusively that the framework of reality that held our allegiance over the past 400 years is inadequate. It is not large enough to account for all of reality. Quantum physics, looking into the mysteries of reality at the level of particles, electrons and atoms, has concluded that reality is one vast, unified singularity, a cosmic web of unity. Something immaterial is holding reality together. Something immaterial is unfolding the material world. Something immaterial is metamorphosing the material world, constantly eroding, altering and removing worn-out old forms and creating new and fresh forms. Reality is continually shape-shifting Itself at the material level. The Something that is so dynamic in reality is the creative force of invisible, living Being. The scientists are not ready to go there yet, but the trend is inevitably in that direction.

The new reality that is dawning on us is that we live in the midst of a mysterious, shimmering Sea of living, conscious creativity and generativity. The consciousness that we use to navigate our way through life every day is an integral part of that Sea of pure consciousness and pure creativity. When we turn inward to perceive our pool of consciousness, we are contacting the living creativity of pure Being itself. The space around us is filled with this livingness and creativity. We are in a vast Field of consciousness, livingness and creativity every moment of our lives. It is time for us to wake up to this fact and realize how astounding we, and the miraculous Field, actually are. It appears that we are now beginning to do that.

4
One Livingness

A pulse is pounding
beneath the world,
beating in regular time,
and as it strikes
its deepest note,
we enter the Sublime.
We are not the point here.
Our miracle is one of many.
The Field of mysterious energy,
the Sea of Life beneath,
is the source of our intensity,
the core of our reality.
Fall on your knees
in wonder,
bow your head in awe.
Open your eyes
to see the Real,
and melt into the Mystery.

There is no death in the universe. There is only endless movement into and out of material form. The Field, a vast arena of sub-atomic particles, eternally clusters or aggregates Itself into forms, holds them in being for a time, then deconstructs and recycles them into new forms. We are observers of a Cosmic process of metamorphosis as the Field reorganizes and shifts Its shape into ever new configurations.

The Field Itself is pure Livingness. It spins off the material realm as a by-product, out of Its restless nature. The Field—that is, the Cosmos—is totally and completely alive. It is the very principle of

Livingness. Material forms come and go within this invisible ocean of Livingness.

When an organic form ceases to function and its particles are deconstructed, we have learned to call that death. The event is laced with fear and foreboding for humans, because they are identified with the material body. They believe that when that goes, everything goes. So, death becomes a great bottomless Abyss, a chasm of emptiness into which we might forever fall.

But, the universe is not empty. It is full. It is a plenum. We know now that space itself, the essence of emptiness, is actually jammed with sub-atomic particles blinking in and out of existence. Space is full of life. Quantum physics has concluded that the universe is a singularity, a "Unified Field." If the universe is only one thing then there is no room for the two categories of the living and the dead. There is only the single category of the life of the unified field.

In a similar way, the distinction that we have made in the past between life and non-life no longer applies. Everything in the material world has life and Being at its core. The wooden chair at your dining room table is as alive, though perhaps in a different degree, as the tree from which it was made or the seed from which the tree germinated.

The criteria that science developed to distinguish life from non-life, criteria such as respiration, elimination, assimilation of food, were all developed in a pre-unity framework. In a world where it is accepted that objects are separate from each other, it makes sense to distinguish the category of living organisms from the category of the inert, non-living material forms. In the new world of the unified field, there are no isolated objects. The Cosmos is a single Field or web of inter-relationship, without any separate parts whatsoever. Everything in that Field is all moving together and shape-shifting into the next configuration. It's all one thing, and It's all alive and laced with sentient Being.

Traditional science is having a little trouble catching up with its own new knowledge in quantum physics. We are witnessing radical and primordial shifts in understanding reality as a result of the new discoveries. For the most part, the traditional scientists are still thinking in terms of the separate forms of the old, eroding world-view. It may take some time for the tradition-bound coterie, which looks backward and has career interests bound up in the old framework, to adjust to the shimmering new universe that is opening before us.

5
Cosmic Awareness

Beneath the skin of the world
a powerful Life resides,
awake and aware,
luminous and shining.
It unfolds Itself
as a vast,
intricate,
patterned Cosmos,
pouring Its
livingness and brilliance
into a waiting world.

The universe is aware. Contrary to the reigning worldview in science, the primary reality in the Cosmos is not material but Consciousness. We live out our lives in a vast matrix of Consciousness. It is the nature of Being. In a real way, Being and Consciousness are the same thing. We have experiences of the Matrix of Consciousness as we go about our daily lives. In Its greatest gift to us, Being has given us access to Its Consciousness. We have only to turn inward and It is there, just behind our eyes.

Quantum physics has proven that the Universe is a singularity, one thing, a "Unified Field," with no separate parts. If there is only one thing here, the Field, and if Consciousness exists anywhere in the Field, as it does in us, then the entire Field must be conscious. There is no place in the Field for Consciousness to be localized. That view comes out of the previous framework of separation. In a Cosmos that is an inseparable web of life and existence, it is not possible that Consciousness is restricted to only a few organic entities such as ourselves. We are floating in an infinite ocean of Consciousness, of which our experience inside our heads is just a miniscule bit.

Traditional science, formed around the separatist frameworks of Newton and Descartes, has for 400 years held that the universe operates like a vast, clock-work machine. The separate parts in that machine collide with each other in space and transfer energy to each other in the collision. This all takes place in empty space, which acts as a simple container for the moving, material parts. There is no place in this equation for a living universe or a conscious universe.

In the past 70 years, however, quantum physics has turned this world-view on its head. Space is not empty, but full of particles popping in and out of existence so fast that our senses cannot perceive them. This has been called "quantum foam." The parts of the universe are not separate from each other but joined absolutely together in a web of unity. The dying Newtonian view that objects collide and transfer energy to each other is limited in its application. It is true at one level of reality, the material level. At a more macro level, there are no separate objects to collide. There is only one Cosmos-sized, invisible Field erupting forth the material realm and shifting its shape. In that metamorphosis, the unfolding spectacle of the physical world appears to our senses.

When a person walks across a room, we are caught in an illusion. There is no room separate from the person. There are not two separate places in the room to move between. There is, at the macro level, only the Cosmos shifting Its shape into a new configuration. It's going to take a while to get our minds around this startling new vision of reality.

The one area that the new framework makes simpler and more understandable is parapsychology. The phenomena of parapsychology—distant viewing, pre-cognition, telepathy, etc.—are all incomprehensible anomalies in the separatist framework. However, in the emerging framework of oneness, they easily make sense.

Telepathy, for example, can be conceived as a matter of leakage or input of one person's thoughts into the Field, picked out of the Field by another person who is also connected to it. Both people are part of the same Sea of Consciousness, each not only connected but integral to the

Sea. Information travels throughout the entire expanse of the Field, and is available at any point in It.

The thrust of human evolution seems to be toward growing a "Hive Consciousness" that will permit the exchange of thoughts without language. Our destiny may be stranger than science-fiction. We unfold too slowly to perceive the changes in our evolution but we can be aware of their general direction.

We live in an extraordinary, transitional time. Our world-view, our fundamental understanding of reality, is shifting rapidly. The old certainties are disappearing from beneath our feet. They served their purpose. They were once the cutting edge of evolution but now they are becoming passé, barriers to our unfolding. They are fast becoming anachronisms.

We are being called upon to enter a new Universe. It is a strange and unfamiliar place, and we don't yet know all of the rules of Its operation. We can't hang onto the tried and the true from the past. We must go forward with open eyes and a certain amount of courage. It's an exciting time to be alive on the earth.

6
The Abyss

Before me lies the Abyss.
I peer into Its depths.
The darkness overwhelms me.
The fear constricts my heart.
What if this Void is living?
What if It's loving me?
What if I could see
the whole of things
and see the miracle
it is to be?

Humans live with fear. Our first experiences in life are of our smallness and vulnerability. As we grow and occasionally are hurt, we become ever more aware of our innate fragility. As adults, we learn to live our lives in spite of fear, but we never lose the awareness that, around the next corner, our time here could end.

A central but over-looked feature of this condition is the Abyss. It is more than a metaphor. It is an intrinsic part of human consciousness. It is experienced by us all.

The Abyss is the feeling, and often the vision, that we are standing on the brink of a bottomless, empty, black void. Further, that we might topple into that void and fall forever into emptiness. It's a terrifying experience, and produces a terrified feeling in the body, a feeling that the bottom has dropped out of your stomach. There is nothing left to hold you. Generally we attempt to repress or turn away from this unpleasant sensation as quickly as possible. We avoid it in dread. However, it resurrects itself continually and comes to us, momentarily, in all stages of life.

The culture's concept of death is, of course, a perfect embodiment of the Abyss. It pictures us disappearing forever into an infinity of emptiness and lifelessness. We almost never investigate the Abyss because we are so busy backpedaling from it. However, it keeps surfacing out of our deepest mind. If we allow ourselves to look at it, however, we find that the main component that is terrifying us is the emptiness, the bottomless emptiness.

The experience of the Abyss is particularly prominent in human experience in our time period, because we have dispensed with the core component of reality—invisible, living Being. We have followed science into the view that the Cosmos is a dead and empty, black void, with only a few living pieces in it, like ourselves. Functioning like a massive, lifeless clockwork machine, the Cosmos itself is considered to be devoid of life. This view of reality makes the Abyss omnipresent. In actuality, it makes the Cosmos into the Abyss. We are expected to live our lives in the midst of this dead, empty space. The results, not surprisingly, are the rampant human experiences of desolation, despair, insignificance, futility, and a kind of on-going sorrow about our lives.

If living Being is added back into the worldview equation, the Abyss transforms itself into boundlessness. The Abyss is the infinity of the universe when viewed by the fearful separateness of the ego. When we perceive from a place of oneness, the Abyss turns into living boundlessness. We know that in facing the universe we are facing infinity. If it is an infinity of emptiness, void and death, it is more than we can handle, and we sink into despair. We lose hope because there is nothing in the universe to hope for, nothing that is innately good and intrinsically positive. It is all just dead, empty void. Oblivion is our present experience and our only destiny.

If, however, the Cosmos is viewed as a conscious, intelligent and evolving Field of livingness, we suddenly find ourselves in a Matrix worth living in. Our little lives are tiny but intrinsic parts in a system of magnificence. We suddenly belong. We are significant, as a part of Something profound, wondrous and positive. When we turn toward the vastness of the night sky, we perceive life and consciousness at the macro-cosmic levels. The

Abyss and the fear that it generates disappear. We are swept into the boundlessness of living Being, magnificent and shimmering.

When living Being is incorporated into the world-view, and the Abyss is transformed into Being's boundlessness, we feel like dropping to our knees in wonder. We suddenly belong to Something mysterious, majestic and eternal. We have come home.

7
Quantum Consciousness

We are not yet
what we will be.
A new kind of mind
is blooming
that will take us
to realms now unseen,
beyond separateness,
beyond isolation,
beyond loneliness and despair,
to the knowledge
that is coming like thunder,
that we and the Cosmos
are one.

In our lifetime, we are surfing a great wave of evolution. It is changing our consciousness and taking us forward into a mysterious and unknown future. When the evolution finally matures, we will scarcely be recognizable as the same human beings.

This has happened before in human history. We have undergone at least three major transformations in our consciousness as a species. Each change added a previously non-existent quality and dimension to our consciousness, and propelled us into new adventures on the planet.

We started with archaic consciousness. This is associated with our animal beginnings. It was simple animal awareness of the self and environment, awareness that enabled life and allowed the species to continue. For millennia, this is what we were.

At some point in pre-history, a new quality bloomed in consciousness. It has been called magical consciousness, and it was contemporaneous with our time in the caves. Humans began to reach tentatively toward realization of cause and effect, trying to influence events and realities with incantations, rites and rituals. They perceived the world as inter-twined and filled with invisible, mysterious, powerful forces that influenced reality. They attempted to intervene and impose their own will on reality, to manipulate these forces to ensure their food sources and survival.

Around 9,000 or 10,000 years ago, another qualitative change occurred. It has been called mythical consciousness. We began to build cities and organize our food resources. We invented agriculture, and language developed exponentially, including writing. Humans began to see themselves and their societies as part of huge, mythical stories playing themselves out against the backdrop of the natural world. They extracted themselves, for the most part, from their previous fusion with nature, and conceptual thinking and rationality began to appear.

Our present stage has been called mental consciousness. It began about 2,500 years ago. It increased the capacities for good thinking and invention, and led eventually to the development of the technologies that today have transformed our world.

We are enchanted now with our progress and inventions, but we lost something along the way. In developing our science and technologies, which focus exclusively on the material realm, we lost the invisible core of reality—living, conscious Being. Being contains in Its nature all the organizing, coherent patterns and principles that we use in our technologies and investigate in our sciences. With this loss of Being, we have become increasingly desolate, in despair, alienated and isolated. This is where we are today.

The Quantum Consciousness that is now blooming may bring some relief. It is rapidly forming a new view of macro-reality, based on the discoveries of quantum physics. We are being challenged to flexibility, to open to entirely new ways of perceiving reality. The old framework is no longer adequate. It is no longer big enough to encompass the new macro-reality that is rapidly appearing in the human mind.

The core of the change is identity. We have seen ourselves as separate little beings, struggling and trying to survive and flourish in a dangerous and threatening world. Our separateness has been unquestioned. It is, after all, the evidence of our physical senses. It is the reality that we perceive. How could things be otherwise?

Now, those assumptions are in question. Perhaps reality is deeper and more complex than our physical senses can discern. In our lifetime, quantum physics has begun unraveling the simple identity of separateness. It has thrown up the astounding truth that we are not separate but enmeshed in a singular, undifferentiated web of Being that is as large as the Cosmos Itself. We and the Cosmos are one thing. There are no separate parts. The universe and everything in it are a singularity. The quantum physicists call this Field of Being the "Unified Field," and they mean exactly that—unity. It is difficult for us to get our minds around this new perspective, particularly in view of what we perceive. It is difficult for even the scientists to absorb it. Many of them are continuing to carry out their experiments based on the old framework of separateness. It may take some time for the implications of the new knowledge about reality to elaborate itself and be integrated.

In the meantime, we can work on our own understanding. What does the unity of the Cosmos mean for us? For starters, it means that the story of the Cosmos, from the Big Bang to our day, is our own story. The unfolding of the universe is one long, undivided, seamless, creative event occurring over a period of 13.7 billion years. Galaxies formed, stars exploded, elemental materials such as carbon and hydrogen were blown through space to become the planets and all the life on them, including us. We are made of stardust. Exploding stars are the only way that carbon enters the universe, and our bodies are composed of carbon.

The story of the Cosmos is our story. Our origin is not with our parents but much farther back—with the Big Bang. We are more than resident in the Cosmos and connected to Its processes. We are the Cosmos Itself, unfolding Its miraculous creativity in new life-forms such as ourselves. We are larger than we thought. We are more miraculous than we thought. We are more integral to the living, shimmering, mysterious Field of Being that is the Cosmos than we thought. We are beginning to live in and experience a fresh, new Universe.

8
The Origins of Art

We stand on the shoulders
of those who have gone before.
Like us,
they were frightened
and struggling,
Like us,
they tried to understand.
Like us,
they looked at the sparkling stars
and the vastness of Living Space,
and felt their hearts
bursting in wonder
to be in this sacred place.

Making art is a quintessentially human pre-occupation. We are the only animals that produce artifacts for purely aesthetic reasons. The impulse to create something new, beautiful and meaningful arises out of the deepest nature of Being. It is Being's creativity that fires the human nervous system with the impulses to create, and organizes those impulses into orchestrated, fruitful activity. Making art is a very strong internal impulse. It impels the human into action, although the goal and end result is hazy and uncertain. True art does not know where it is headed. By definition, it is seeking to produce something completely original, something that has never existed before. This is one of the most exciting, compelling, rewarding activities that a human being can undertake. It is also one of the most mysterious, as it throws the human consciousness into a partnership of co-creation with Being. Imbued with the experience of touching into the deepest nature of

Being and Its unfolding, making art totally absorbs the attention. It is an addictive activity.

Art was born out of terror. Humans began to make art about 40,000 years ago, during our time in the caves. This was the Paleolithic period, when the glaciers moved down into Europe, receded, and moved down again. This happened four times, producing four ice ages. Human survival hung in the balance. Conditions were beyond extreme. Cold, starvation, animals, disease, infection and accident were daily threats. Life was brutal and filled with fear.

The Paleolithic culture was a hunting and gathering life. The continuation of life depended on finding food sources. There was an on-going crisis around food. If you couldn't find food for a few days, then you might become too weak to hunt, and the whole group might perish. The major sources of food were the animal herds that grazed on the plains of Europe. The very survival of these people depended on those animals. They felt themselves intimately linked to the animals. The animals were considered to be divine, to have souls, and to be an integral part of a great chain of life.

The connection between humans and animals was a central feature of that chain. The humans desperately needed the animals to be available for the kill. They developed what we now call Totemism, the belief that the human was inextricably linked at the soul level with the animal. It was in this context that art was born. In an attempt to mobilize every possible resource to enable the continuation of their life, these people developed rites, rituals and incantations to keep the animals coming to them. They believed that the animals were voluntarily offering themselves to be killed for the benefit of the humans. Continued success of this pattern depended on being appreciative of this sacrifice, this gesture of selflessness by the animals.

As part of these rites, men began to make pictures of animals and the hunt on the cave walls. They were magical pictures. They most probably depicted the successful outcomes of future hunts, and perhaps thanksgiving for hunts already successfully completed. This was a deadly serious game. By making these images, the people of the caves were attempting to intervene in reality, to mobilize unseen forces to assist them in the hunt. It was probably the earliest dim reaching toward the principle of cause and effect. They were attempting through magic to become the cause of the effect that they desired.

They also believed that the animal, once killed, was reborn. They lived in a cosmology of constant rebirth, rebirth not only for man but for all the animals on which their survival depended. The entire process was divine but, as Joseph Campbell has noted, they were drenched in blood as a way of life. Their lives depended on continual killing. Their rites, rituals and beliefs served to make all this endurable. A contemporary Eskimo has said that the greatest peril of life lies in the fact that human food consists entirely of souls.

Out of this cosmology of killing, based on fear of annihilation, art was born. One definition of art is "to embody the unseen, to make visible in the world that which exists only in the inner world." This definition applies equally to the ancient people and modern man. In order for magic to work, everything must be invisibly interconnected. A rite done over here will not affect reality over there unless there is an unseen but effective connection. The reality of unseen connection that sustained us in the caves is reappearing in our consciousness today. The unified field of quantum physics that regards the universe as a single web of inter-connection tracks almost exactly the magical Paleolithic attitude toward unseen connections in reality. After 40,000 years, perhaps we are circling back to a core truth of reality—a cosmology of total connection. After our voyage into separateness of 40,000 years, perhaps we are headed back toward oneness. Throughout all that time, art has been a spiritual activity of humans. Born in terror, it was in its origins and still is today an attempt to participate in invisible reality.

9
Mythos and Logos

My consciousness
is the mind of the Great One,
awake, alive, aware,
a Field of Sensitivity
that is loaned to me
for just this very short span of time.
I can feel Its vastness.
I can feel Its depth.
I bathe in Its brilliant light.
Perhaps the purpose of this may be
to enable me to see
the meaning that is surrounding me
in the patterns of the Cosmos.

Humans are organisms that exist in two mental realms. The first realm is a realm of inner images that is in place when we are born. The little child is primarily in touch with these inner images rather than the outer world. We can see this as we watch a child play by itself or with other children. They create scenarios and characters in their heads that are completely real to them, as real or more real than the outer world. The focus on this inner realm is completely natural to children, and they constantly express their inner experience as they develop.

This inner realm has been labeled in many ways. It has been called the imagination, the realm of inner images, the creative realm. It can also be described as the Mithal or the realm of Mythos. Mythos is a term from anthropology. It is a way of understanding the world that was ascendant in earlier periods of human history. It is interested in the meaning that lies beneath the material world, and it relies on images, metaphors and myths to understand what it all means. The myths of the ancient peoples were much more than entertainment. They were products of a particular kind of mind that was current at the time. The myths were used as tools for interpreting and understanding human life and the universe, the timeless and eternal, and the origins, connections and nature of life. The myths also provided models of ideal behavior for the individuals in those cultures. Mythos is very closely connected to creativity. Both creativity and Mythos emerge from the unconscious mind, and the language of both is primarily imagery.

The second kind of human mind, the opposite of Mythos, is Logos. We all know about Logos because today we are firmly in the grip of this way of thinking. It is rational and pragmatic. It is rooted in language. It pays attention primarily to the material world. It is good for practical matters, such as insurance policies, retirement plans, and career decisions. It is the mind for functioning in the world. It operates in a linear way, and it is concerned with being effective and efficient and successful in the world. Logos can also be called the material mind, the outer mind, the mind of the world, the practical mind, the rational mind, or the mind of reason. Logos is necessary for figuring out how to survive and flourish in the world. What Logos cannot do is to produce meaning. Our sense of meaning in life comes from a very deep place in consciousness that has nothing to do with bank accounts or notoriety or fame or success in our profession. Our sense of meaning comes from the depths of the mind, the place of Mythos. We can see about us successful, rich and famous people whose lives are so empty and unsatisfactory that they commit suicide. It happens all the time. So, Logos is very important to human welfare for taking care of business, and Mythos is very important to human welfare for having meaning and depth in our consciousness.

In our culture, Logos has become so dominant that Mythos has almost disappeared. The realm of Mythos has atrophied in us. It is inaccessible or nonexistent in many people today, and as a result their lives have lost depth and meaning. Deprived of significance, humans fall easily into despair. Logos is all about facts. Most deep truths about life cannot be understood from the bare facts, with Logos. The question of Mythos is not "What happened?" but "What does it mean?" The deepest questions of life are Mythos in nature, and harvesting their meaning is not available except to a mind thinking in the Mythos mode.

The truth of the matter is that we need both of these ways of thinking in order to live fulfilled lives. We need Logos with its rational, linear, good thinking to handle our affairs in the world, and we need the depth, meaning and intuitive connections that come with Mythos in order to experience and savor the deep qualities of being alive. We are beings of two realms, Logos and Mythos, and we must pay equal attention to each of those realms.

In growing up, most people smack into the world when they reach their teens. It is a harsh adjustment, and at this time a basic conflict arises. That conflict is: "How do I adjust myself to the world, and at the same time retain the richness of my inner world?" This is a very difficult question to resolve, because the world is so demanding. The scales are heavily weighted in favor of Logos. Survival fears are triggered, and young people wonder how they will ever manage to make a place for themselves in what is obviously a very harsh, demanding world.

People respond to this question in individual ways. Some people proceed to give up Mythos completely, and turn their attention exclusively to the tasks of getting educated, making a living and becoming successful in the society. This choice looks attractive and even necessary, but it usually leads to a life that is a busy rat-race without much depth or meaning. There is no time for depth and meaning because the material demands are coming so fast and furiously, are constantly expanding and are so pressing that they take all the time and energy available. The people who choose Logos exclusively at the expense of Mythos are candidates for burn-out in middle age. They may also become bored with what they're doing in life, even if they are successful at it. They run a real risk of watching their inner life dry up, or watching their interests and consciousness increasingly become trapped into smallness. By making the choice exclusively for Logos, they cut themselves off from the deep wellsprings of the human spirit. Those wellsprings are the source of our renewal and refreshment. They are crucial to our long-term health and happiness. Sooner or later in the life of the exclusively Logos person, the consequences and costs of the loss of access to these deep wellsprings will emerge in their outer life. It is well worth the time and effort to keep Mythos alive in our consciousness.

Other people (we usually call them artists) handle the question by opting primarily for the imaginative life, the creative life, sometimes at the expense of Logos. Their attention and energy are taken up with the excitement and contemplation of their inner images, their creative projects, the Mythos realm of their consciousness. These people can be very deficient in taking care of the practical problems of life because they pay so little attention to them. They look at the practical, material side of life only when absolutely forced to do so, and sometimes not even then. Questions such as insurance and retirement plans are distasteful to them, and so they do not address the issues. This exclusively Mythos person runs the risk of creating serious crises in their life by failing to address the problems that require thought and prior planning.

The solution to this problem of harmonizing the inner and outer realms is to realize that we are simultaneously beings of both realms. Each realm must be attended to or we will suffer negative consequences. The realm of Logos must be given attention so that the basic problems of life are addressed and taken care of—making a living, taking care of business, raising children, and creating some kind of security. The realm of Mythos must be given attention in order to have access to a rich inner life of depth and meaning. It is difficult to hold the two realms in mind at the same time. One possibility is to alternate in attending to them. At the least, we must hold in our conscious awareness the necessity to nurture and attend to both realms.

If Mythos is lacking in our life, it can be amplified by intentionally choosing a creative project that is not related to outer success. If it is aimed at success, or proving ourselves exceptional, then Mythos will be co-opted by Logos and turned into a vehicle of planning, rational goals and self-promotion. If we choose a creative project simply to bring Mythos back into our life, and not to make ourselves successful and admired, then our unconscious will come forward and support the project. Once engaged, the unconscious will begin to supply our waking consciousness with images and ideas that relate to the project.

We may begin to dream about it. Images and ideas connected to it may suddenly appear while we are cooking or washing dishes or taking a shower. The purpose here is to work with great awareness with the stream of imagery floating up from the depths of our unconscious mind. If this begins to happen, then we will know that we are engaged in something important, something far more important than pursuing a little hobby. We will be opening up another realm of mind, a deeper layer of consciousness that may have lain neglected for a long while, a realm that is crucial to the fullness and satisfaction of our lives. We call it creativity, but we could as well call it wholeness.

10
The Journey of the Soul

We spend our lives
trying to figure out
how to get value
and be O.K.
What if we're already there?
What if value was conferred on us
at the moment of our birth?
We have been plucked
from the Void
to walk this splendid Earth
as a human being
for just a short span of time,
the latest model
of this marvelous creature,
fifteen billion years
in the making,
now the Cosmos
in human form.
This is our value.

There are three relationships that we need to tend simultaneously in our lives. The first relationship is with ourselves. We have an inner environment. We live with it every moment that we are conscious. That relationship with ourselves is ongoing and continuous and needs to be carefully tended. Second, we have a relationship with the group, with other people. We are social animals. Humans are very engaged with how they look to the group, how they are treated by the group, their status in the group, their standing with other people. The relationship with the group needs to be tended continuously. The third relationship is with the Cosmos. This is the most important of the three.

If we have a decent, ongoing, accessible contact with Being, with the Cosmos, we can weather life. We can get through the hard things, survive them and keep going. We will not be plunged into permanent, irredeemable despair. If we are shut off from Being and thrown back on the resources of our little, limited and pretty incapable organisms, we will be in trouble. The separate little human is not strong enough and powerful enough to cope with life. It's not an easy thing to be a human being. We are vulnerable. We are fearful. We have difficult events hitting us, burning us and pounding us. We have to keep going somehow. If we have no access to Being and we have not tended that relationship, if in fact we don't understand that there is a substratum of Livingness beneath the material world that is throwing us up and creating us moment to moment, we will not have the strength and support to live our lives fully. We will suffer despair and desolation. We will be shut off from the Source of our life. We will be shut off from everything that is sacred, deep and meaningful. There is no remedy for that place of desolation except to get in touch with Being. The Sufis call that state of desolation and alienation 'Sha'qa.' The state of nearness to Being, of having your organism irrigated with its gifts of joy, optimism and well-being, is called 'Sa'ada.'

The Journey of the Soul is the Sufi answer to why we are here on Earth. It envisions a kind of contractual relationship with Being. It starts with the presumption, either metaphoric or in reality, that between lives you make a contract with Being about where you're going to be born, the parents you're going to be born to, and the circumstances and issues that you're going to deal with in your upcoming life. This includes issues that you are going to have to cope with as you travel the arc of your next human life. So, life is conceived as a search for the reason that you came to Earth, and what you were intended to do while here.

The Journey of the Soul begins at the moment of birth. It is a journey orchestrated around the Soul Contract. It's a journey about the unfolding of our potential. It's a journey of maturation. It's a journey of education and development that occurs while working our way back to Being. The life arc is viewed as a circle. We start from Being, progress through our childhood, adulthood and old age and then return to Being. All the way through, we are aware at some deep level that we are working our way back to Being. In the process of trying to find our way back to Being, we have the opportunity to express the potential that we came here to express as part of our Soul Contract.

The Sufis have taken this idea of life as a journey, a maturation process, and divided it into seven stages. They call these seven stages Nafs. The word Nafs means soul. The architecture of this idea is lovely. The concept is that each Nafs is a separate kind of soul. In the process of living, as you refine the soul, it moves into new stages of development. Through this refining process, the soul can see more of reality. It has a clearer view of Spirit. It is closer to Being. It is less invested in itself, less self-absorbed. It moves to higher planes of existence and development. In those higher plane, it exists as a different kind of soul. One way of saying this is that the soul metabolizes its experiences and is transformed. The metabolization, the learning and the new and larger vision of reality all change its nature and its consciousness. If consciousness is changed, then one acts differently. One has a different framework and a different perspective on life, so the shift can be seen from the outside. To some extent, at least to people who know what they are looking for, the Nafs currently occupied is recognizable. The level of soul development is apparent.

11
The First Nafs

The veils are tight around me.
They close my eyes.
They shrink my mind.
I find it impossible to see
the beauty of the world.
Yet, I know it is still there.
This is all inside me.
I will be still and silent
and wait until I
can once again see
the miracle that it is
to be.

The first Nafs is where we all begin. It is called the Depraved Nafs. It is the lowest common denominator of souls. If you have done a great deal of work on yourself in previous lifetimes, you may be born into this life at a higher Nafs. The First Nafs is called in the West the ego. Each higher Nafs is attained by work and previous realizations. We are working our way to greater and greater refinement of the soul, but there is no guarantee of progress. There is no guarantee that we're going to succeed in the refining process. At any stage it is possible to revert back to a previous stage. We can even revert from a very advanced stage clear back to the very first Nafs. Sometimes we see spiritual teachers doing exactly that. They lose their way and begin acting out in ways that they should know better. In such cases, the First Nafs has been re-entered.

The soul learns not by thinking about life and reality but by actually experiencing things. The soul almost always has to go through experiences in order to learn lessons about what to avoid, pathways not to follow. People can learn from looking at other's mistakes, but they must be very alert to do so.

In a sense, the theory of Nafs envisions changing our identity as the soul is refined. We move up the ladder into higher and higher Nafs. We are changing who we are, who and what we take ourselves to be. At any given time, we occupy a particular station in the ascending ladder of refinement, and this station can be seen by others, as least by those who know what to look for. The soul is working its way slowly back to Being. In the process, it is expanding its frame of reference and increasing its understanding of the nature of the Cosmos, the nature of the human being, and the relationship between the two. There is greater understanding of Core Reality as one moves successively from Nafs to Nafs. There is deeper and more gounded vision.

The First Nafs is an undeveloped, simple, primate consciousness. We know this one very, very well. Some people may stay in this Nafs for their whole lives. There is no guarantee that you will move beyond this level. If you don't bother to work on yourself spiritually, you will almost certainly stay stuck at this level. This is the most primitive kind of Nafs. It's consciousness is common. The person is wholly entrapped in worldly pursuits, in contact only with the material world and completely self-absorbed. He or she is almost entirely unconscious of Being, and not really interested in invisible realities. He or she is suffering, lonely, desolate, unhappy, and looking desperately for some kind of relief. He or she is also unsupported by Being. In the framework there is no place for Being, so there is no access to Being. This produces a constant state of fear, which can range from mild to intense.

This is a superficial consciousness. There appear to be no deeper realms. The mental energy in this kind of individual is used mostly to solve problems. As we know, as quickly as we solve one problem and it disappears, another takes its place.

This process can go on for a lifetime, so that you really don't do anything with your mind except solve problems, one after the other. That's the pattern of the first Nafs. There is little time in the life of the person of the first Nafs to feel wonder, to raise the head and look at the Cosmos. There is no appreciation whatsoever of the miracles of life that are operating to keep us on this Earth every second that we are here. This kind of person is totally pre-occupied with status and material things. At bottom, they feel valueless and deficient. This leads them to desperately claw at the world, to try to get some kind of value, under the mistaken impression that having things or success will solve the problem. They are always coming out of a sense of deep deficiency because they are not in touch with Being, the only place that would give them a sense of value. They are clawing at the world to get status, to get value, to be recognized, to be seen, to be appreciated in some way. They don't know how to get what they need, but material things, achievement or fame seem like possibilities. The first Nafs is the false self or the ego, recognized by all the wisdom traditions. Above all, it is characterized by blaming others. Whatever goes wrong is always somebody else's fault. In the first Nafs, the person is always a victim of life.

The child development theorists have done us a terrific service by mapping out the development of the child between one and four. In the process, they have mapped the creation of the false self. The most important time in the development of life is between one and four. Immediately after birth, the child experiences the world as an undifferentiated matrix--a sea of unity of light and sound and moving forms. There are no distinctions between self and other. A little later, the child begins to distinguish between self and object. A later stage is dual unity, where the child recognizes that there are two, Mom and me, but there is still a sense of a unity underlying the duality. A little later, the child begins to separate itself and truly distinguish between itself and the mother. The sense of self has emerged. Still later, the child reaches a stage called 'object constancy,' where the environment and every thing in it stabilizes. It knows that the world is out there and I'm in here, and it all stays in place, even when I'm not looking.

At this point, the child begins to be truly functional as a human being. There is orientation and sufficient development of the brain so that the child can cope with the realities of everyday experience. The map of child development is a map of the growth of the ego.

The development of the false self is part biologic and part psychological. This development creates two experiences. One of them is the experience of separateness. The other is a sense of identity. Identity can be defined as the unique set of characteristics that distinguish you in your own mind from everybody else. And, of course, it is the answer to the questions 'Who am I?', or "What am I?"

The goal of spiritual work is to broaden the framework and loosen the hold of the ego. The ego's hold on your consciousness must be loosened in order to move beyond separateness. You have to loosen that hold in order to truly open to the expansiveness of Being and experience 'Sa'ada', nearness to Being. When you are in a state of 'Sa'ada', the qualities of Being move though and irrigate the nervous system. This creates experiences that include joy, peace, depth, meaning, beauty, value, sacredness, belonging, miraculousness, acceptance, surrender and eternity. That's just a beginning of the list. In the state of 'Sa'ada,' it is wonderful just to be alive.

That's what we want in our lives. The only place to go to get those qualities flowing through your nervous system is Being. We cannot get it from a new red car. What we can get from a new red car is about a five minute high, after which you go right back to where you were.

The First Nafs is where we begin the Journey of the Soul. This is what we are all engaged in by being on the earth as human beings and abiding in a material body. We are all making this journey, ascending slowly to higher levels of refinement through experience, maturation and hard knocks. We are moving through the successive stages of the soul, the Nafs, and we are headed ultimately back toward Being.

12
The Second Nafs

I swim in unfolding Majesty,
while I'm doubting
my value and worth.
I'm suffused
with Shimmering Life,
while I'm pondering
my lack of success.
The Universe flares Its wonders
while I stew myself
in my fears.
Surely to God,
as evolving humans,
we can do better than this.

The Sufis see The Journey of the Soul on earth as a progression through a series of seven stages that they call Nafs. Each successive Nafs involves a refinement of the soul. Each is, in effect, a different kind of soul as a result of its previous learnings. As we move through the Nafs, we are progressively less self absorbed, more awake and aware, and more focused on ultimate Reality, which is Being.

The first Nafs is the most primitive soul, characterized by blaming others for our problems. It is a state of victimhood, undeveloped and unrefined, totally self-referential, and fixated on the material level of existence. It rarely or never raises its head to perceive the splendor of the Cosmos or the miracles happening all around us. Living in the first Nafs is the experience of a superficial bardo.

The Second Nafs is a little improvement on the first Nafs, but not much. It is also characterized by blame. However, at this stage one ceases to blame others and starts to blame oneself. The soul at this stage of development is in a mode of self-attack. The Second Nafs is still pretty primitive and undeveloped. It also sees only a tiny, limited portion of reality.

With the Second Nafs, we are in the territory of what psychology calls the Super-ego. Modern depth psychology, arising out of the work of Freud and Jung, defines the Super-ego as the internalized parents. As a child, we are corrected and disciplined by our parents. Their attention to us in this regard is a socializing influence. They attempt to teach us who and how to be, in order to fit into the culture. They exercise a controlling influence on us, a teaching function.

Later, after leaving the parents, the adult child retains their voices and instructions in his/her head. It is the job of the Super-ego to keep us in line. When we consider straying beyond the bounds of the normal and healthy, the Super-ego will raise objections and resistance, and struggle with us to keep us virtuous. If necessary, it will inflict shame on us to warn us away from unhealthy avenues. If we persist in our plans and carry out the unwise plans, it will plant shame so firmly around the subject that we feel it for the rest of our lives. This basic job of the Super-ego is healthy and necessary. If we were not held back by its socializing messages, there might be a great many more sociopaths in the world.

However, in some people the Super-ego gets out of control and begins to launch attacks on the psyche. It becomes a cruel inner critic, with messages that can range from mild self-criticism to vicious, devastating, self-esteem-destroying, all-out vilification. With continuous messages of deficiency, it can destroy peace of mind, will, satisfaction in life and self-esteem. It can make life totally miserable. It has no dearth of subject matter. Its messages can run the gamut: "You're fat and unattractive." "You're old and washed up." "No-one wants you." "You're stupid."

With its continuous stream of invective, it can turn life into a veritable hell. It is made more difficult by the fact that its messages are usually accepted without question as truth. It appears as a whisper in the mind, and seems to confirm one's worst fears. And, it usually seizes on a subject that has a kernel of truth in it. However, the deficiency or inadequacy that is the heart of its message is greatly amped up, so that it becomes devastating, especially if the message comes several times a day.

The key to dealing with a super-ego attack is to recognize the attack and fight back in our mind. The Super-ego must be regarded as an entity in our psyche that is inimical to our welfare. We must train ourselves to register the attack the moment the Super-ego launches it, then swing into a counter-attack. We must come back at the Super-ego with energy equal to the energy of its attack. We must defend ourselves with statements such as: "Get out of my head." "Take a powder." "Buzz off." It is no good to get into an argument with the Super-ego about whether its message is true. It must be energetically dismissed. A little profanity helps add energy to the defense. We must try to defend consistently, every time the Super-ego launches an attack. In time, the attacks will come less frequently and less viciously.

Using this method of defending, some people are able finally, with great relief, to silence the Super-ego completely. The Super-ego cannot thrive in the daylight. It is powerful only as a whisper from deep in the mind, accepted without question as truth. Once it is identified, objectified, and pulled out into the open, it loses its power. It loses its ability to devastate. It is reduced to a simple voice in the mind, coming from an enemy who is not out for your welfare, and without any ultimate truth.

The Second Nafs, centered on wrestling with the Super-ego, is an uncomfortable place to live. By understanding and moving past the Super-ego's attacks and messages of deficiency and inadequacy, we open the way to the Third Nafs, where real refinement of the soul begins to take place.

13
The Third Nafs

Lift your eyes.
Open your mind.
Expand your conscious view.
A whole new world,
a whole new Cosmos
is waiting just for you.
We're growing up.
We're coming to see
that a living Cosmos
surrounds us here,
a living Sea of Infinity.

The Sufis see the Journey of the Soul as a progression through the Nafs, seven stages of refinement of the soul, maturation, growing through the process of living and growing through the process of hard knocks. The first Nafs, called the "Depraved Nafs" is self-absorbed, unaware for the most part of Being, and characterized by blaming others and a sense of victimization. People can stay in the first Nafs for their entire life. There's no guarantee that one is ever going to move out of it. It takes some spiritual work on ourselves to move.

The second Nafs is also about blame, but it's characterized by blaming oneself. We stop blaming other people but we transfer the impulse to blame to ourselves. It is the Nafs of the Super-ego attack, the infliction of inadequacy and deficiency upon ourselves.

It is with the third Nafs that the soul begins its refinement into true transformation. The third Nafs is called the "Inspired Nafs". For the first time in its maturation process, the soul moves beyond blame. It reaches a higher framework. It's a very important step in refining the soul. It's not the final goal but it's a very, very significant change. It's a step in transforming the soul that allows you to live from a different place. It changes behavior and it changes one's understanding of life, other people and oneself. Many people reach the third Nafs and never go any further. Their life is much better for having reached the third Nafs. It brings a larger framework, a higher perspective to life than that of the first two Nafs. One begins to see the whole pattern of human life, how and why people are reactive, struggling, caught in chaos, and desperately seeking solutions for their suffering. It becomes possible to see this all around us and also in ourselves. In the third Nafs, we quit blaming other people because we become able to see more than one narrative. If we are in the third Nafs and are caught in conflict with someone, we can see their point of view and their rational for their position. We may not agree with it. It may be absolutely contrary to the way that we're seeing the situation, but we can see how their perceptions make sense to them. We are aware that they are coming out of a particular life history and have their own unique and individual window on reality. We know that they can only act out of the givens of their own psyche. The third Nafs allows us to begin to see into people and understand them in all their humanness, even if they're presently posing a problem for us.

The third Nafs also brings increased compassion. It realizes, perhaps not consciously, that every human being is acting in ways that make perfect sense to them. We don't expect them to be just like us, and we don't expect that they're going to reach the same conclusions about life and situations that we reach. We know that they are looking at reality through their own unique window. They're coming to their own judgments about life. They are having their own set of perceptions. Knowing that, we cut them a bit of slack. In the third Nafs, we can perceive that all human beings are trying to protect themselves, get some kind of status and be appreciated. An enormous amount of human behavior is generated by these three goals: to protect oneself, obtain status and be appreciated.

The third Nafs also realizes consciously that all human beings are afraid. We are all operating out of fear. We don't know what's going to happen next. It's difficult to be a human being. We have to keep going with our life and keep pushing into the unknown our entire life. That's what it is to be human. In addition, all human beings are confused. We are all stumbling through life looking for the right path, not knowing how to find that path. In our stumbling and searching, we are having a life. Somebody said, "Life is what happens between cups of tea." Each person is on a very unique individual journey of the soul. Their decisions and responses to life are in accord with that very individual journey. It is not like anybody else's journey. It may make absolutely no sense to an outsider. Looking at someone else's life, we may wonder how they are reaching their decisions. It's perfectly obscure to other people how a particular journey is unfolding, but it's not obscure to the person concerned. Their soul is unfolding itself, sometimes into dark avenues. In trying to find its path, one can get into addictions, one can get into neurosis, one can go quite a long way toward self-destructive behavior before the soul says, "This is not the path. This is not what I'm supposed to be doing. I think I had better back up, try again and go a different direction." That is a very important thing, of course, the ability of the soul to realize, "This is not it. This is a mistake. This is not giving me what I need and making me happy and content. It's leading me exactly the other direction." So, we see people self-correcting all the time. Their soul tries something out and then says, "No, thank you. I don't want to go that direction." The Journey of the Soul is not a straight line. It is a wandering, a meandering, looking for the correct path. It is trying out things. It is trying out life. This is how the soul learns. It actually tries things out. The soul doesn't learn by sitting around and thinking about things. When you sit around and try to think about life, the future is always invisible. We cannot see what is going to happen. We cannot know for sure even what is happening in the present. We can look at the past and see a little bit of what was happening in the past because it's already completed. We can try, perhaps, to see the patterns in our life, but it's very difficult to see the patterns in the present and impossible to see the patterns in the future, because the future can go in any direction. It's full of unexpressed potential which can take any one of many, many paths.

The soul is fumbling its way forward without a map of the territory of life. It does not know its own nature. It does not know what it is trying to do. It does not know its goal. It does not know how to find its path. That is one basic definition of life--the soul trying to find its rightful path through the arc of a life. Some fortunate people, perhaps as a result of previous work on themselves, in many lifetimes perhaps, will stumble upon their path early, even as a child. Einstein, for instance. Einstein had plenty of problems as a young person, but he determined his path fairly early. When people are fortunate enough to do that, the avenue of their life unfolds in front of them. They can focus themselves and go for decades, making a fantastic contribution to human life in pushing into the unknown. We all benefit from the lives of those kinds of people. However, most of us are not like that. Most of us are fumbling and flailing all the way through. We're doing the best we can with the limited understanding that we have.

This is the point, perhaps, to remember the Daimon. The Daimon is the companion that comes with us through our life and remembers what our soul task is, what our soul path is, why we came, and how it is we are supposed to grow. The Daimon is always with us as a source of knowledge about all of those questions. However, it is in the unconscious mind and can't actually be reached. It can reach us, in dreams, impulses and in corrections in behavior. When we note a self-correcting impulse, it is pretty certain that it is the Daimon that is nudging us, pushing us and saying, "Don't do that. Do something else."

Pain is built into the process of living. It's painful to be a human being. There are no human beings who are exempt. The soul is learning lessons from this pain. We're in a crucible here in the alchemical sense. The alchemists used a crucible to burn, pound, throw acids on and cook up things. They were hoping to find the Philosopher's Stone, to find the chemical combinations that would turn base metal into gold. As Jung discovered, that was a metaphor for turning base consciousness into transcendent consciousness that is aware of invisible realities. That is how we are going through our lives. We are trying to turn our base consciousness, which is mostly asleep, into wide-open, wide awake consciousness which is in touch with Reality, the reality of the human being, the reality of the Cosmos and the interaction between the two. With those three subjects, we have pretty well covered the nature of being alive, the nature of Reality. That's what we are trying to do, whether we are aware of it or not. We are trying to grow into our maturity, and refine ourselves so that our consciousness broadens to the point where our consciousness and the Cosmos are one. That's the end goal of the processes of moving through the Nafs. That's where we are all headed eventually.

The question of the third Nafs is not "Why me?" or "Who did this to me?" The questions of the third Nafs are, "What am I supposed to be learning here?" or, "What is the Cosmos trying to teach me by taking me through this hard experience?" Those are the ways that the third Nafs moves past blaming other people. It moves past blaming itself (second Nafs) because it develops compassion for itself. It realizes that "I'm just a human being like everybody else. I am struggling. I don't have a map of life or a playbill. Like everyone else, I have been sent into life without any instructions."

If we begin to develop compassion for ourselves, and allow ourselves to be human, to make mistakes, even bad mistakes, and to be imperfect, a lovingkindness can arise toward ourselves. We can stop attacking ourselves. We cut ourselves some slack for being human and being in the situation of not knowing what to do next, ever. We can begin to develop a warm and tender inner environment for ourselves. We live every waking moment with our inner environment. It's in the walls of our mind. There is a state that characterizes our personal inner environment. It can be very harsh. We can constantly nag ourselves or beat up on ourselves, in which case we're going to go through life coping with a hostile environment in our minds. Or, we can move to a place where we're tender with ourselves, where we treat ourselves with lovingkindness. That's a wonderful place to live from. Since our mental environment is so integral, and is with us every waking moment, it's worth doing some work on our interiority to get to a place where we are compassionate with ourselves. That becomes possible in the third Nafs. It is not possible in the first or second Nafs because they are so focused on blame. In the third Nafs, we move beyond blame and there's an unfolding possibility of creating lovingkindness and tenderness for ourselves and for other people. Harshness and criticism of other people and for ourselves are relaxed.

The third Nafs also begins to develop qualities of patience, perseverance, wisdom, and humility. It provides a larger framework in which to operate. There is a bigger screen of life. It's a natural thing that, in the third Nafs, one would become more patient and more humble and that wisdom could appear because one is not so trapped in the ego. There's an increasing experience of Sa'ada (nearness to being). What that looks like in the third Nafs are moments when we feel our edges dissolve, leaving us suddenly in contact with the livingness of the Universe. We are living our lives in an immense Sea of Livingness. The only thing that keeps us from accessing the immense energy of that Livingness are the mental barriers that we carry. We are also in a state of semi-sleep, unaware of the miracles around us.

Guilt and shame begin to be left behind in the third Nafs. One is progressively moving into a place that is neutral with regard to guilt and shame, because the patterns of human life are better understood, accepted and factored in. Tolerance begins to emerge. Guilt and shame are at the opposite pole from tolerance. We become more tolerant of ourself and others, and we don't feel guilty about our own errors. There is more tolerance for being wrong and mistaken. We just pick up the pieces and say, "I'll try to do better next time." We learn from the experience.

In the third Nafs, the soul occasionally has experiences of feeling brand new. It doesn't matter what our chronological age is. We can be 95 years old and feel absolutely fresh and new. There are also occasional experiences of inspiration. We are more open to the Universe than earlier, and as a result there is an increased feeling of general well-being. This is an integral part of Sa'ada. As we move closer to Being in the refinement of our soul, our nervous system is irrigated with the gifts of Being--joy, peace, clarity, strength, power, creativity, and other essential qualities. Life feels increasingly positive, lovely and rewarding. There is the growing feeling that the world is a wonderful place for a human being, a wonderful place for a soul to experience. With all these changes in our consciousness, the third Nafs changes behavior. Its effects can be observed by the people around us. We begin to act out of a more refined, more compassionate and more understanding soul, and so we treat people differently.

This is what it is to move into the third Nafs. It is a great step in the refinement process, a long way from being the final step, but perhaps the most important breaking point in the long process of developing the Nafs. The first two Nafs are pretty much torture chambers. With movement into the third Nafs, we break free of a very confined reality system. We break into a larger reality, a more Cosmic reality. We understand and experience more of Reality. The movement from the second to the third Nafs is the most dramatic and dynamic movement in all of the journey through the Nafs.

14
The Nafs Four to Seven

I feel an Invisible Majesty
in the space that's all around me,
a Majesty that is boiling
with boundless creativity.
The Sun explodes in fire,
the galaxy slowly turns its wheel,
the planets whirl their endless dance,
all results of this generativity.
Everywhere I turn
I sense the invisible Source,
the vastness of Its mind,
the limitlessness of Its force.
I am struck,
minute by minute,
with the depth of Its infinite mystery.
It is throwing up the Cosmos.
It is throwing up the galaxy.
It is throwing up the Earth,
and in this very moment,
It is throwing up the little me.

By refining the soul, we move through the seven Nafs, the levels of soul development. After the major transformation that is involved in the move from the second Nafs to the third Nafs, the remaining Nafs, four to seven, progressively expand the developments begun in the third Nafs. In the fourth Nafs, there is increasingly less self-absorption. From habitually circling around ourselves, lost in consciousness that is totally self-referential, and seeing everything from the standpoint of ourselves, the person moving into the fourth Nafs begins to expand the screen of awareness. They begin to raise their head from time to time to regard the miraculous Cosmos that has been there, unnoticed, all along.

They also begin to have experiences that are not related to problems. The primate consciousness is primarily concerned with problems, one after the other. As fast as we solve one problem, another rises to the top of the list. It is possible to spend our entire life focused exclusively on problems. In the fourth Nafs, there is a growing awareness that there is a great deal of life that is beyond problem-solving. There is the beginning of a sense of wonder about life and the Cosmos. This sense of wonder and miraculousness will expand in the subsequent Nafs.

The fourth Nafs is called the "Serene Nafs." The ego is diminishing, and consciousness is expanding as a result. The widening of the perceptual screen that began in the third Nafs continues, and there is a deepening of life experience. There is an increasing experience of Sa'ada (nearness to Being), and much less experience of Sha'qa (distance from Being) Trapped in Sha'qa, the qualities of Being do not flow through and irrigate our nervous systems, so there are few or no feelings of joy, wonder, sacredness or miraculousness. The experiences are primarily of despair, desolation, alienation, and feeling cut off from the depth and meaning in life. Sha'qa is a bardo. It's a terrible place to be. As we move through the Nafs, we increasingly leave Sha'qa behind and our experience is increasingly that of the well-being of Sa'ada. As a result, perhaps, of the increasing experience of Sa'ada, there are blooming feelings of generosity. There is the beginning of an impulse to give ourselves, our energy and our capacities, to other people, to humanity. There is the feeling that we possess a potential that we want to somehow give to others. We may not have a vehicle to realize this emerging generosity, but the general impulse can send us on the search for a way to realize it in the world.

The fourth Nafs also carries a new and growing blooming of gratitude. It is a gratitude that feels mixed with wonder, a gratitude for just having been allowed to be alive as a human being. It's a great, very complex, very stunning experience to be on the earth as a human being, and we should continually realize that. We should be grateful all the time. A kind of contentment begins to emerge in the fourth Nafs, a sense of satisfaction with our station in life, whatever it may be. So, we didn't get to be the big deal in life. We have just lived an ordinary little life, and it's great. It's fine. It's enough. There is a growing experience of satisfaction and acceptance of our actual, lived experience.

Along with satisfaction, we begin to bear our hardships with more grace, realizing that they are part of the package deal of being human. Hardship happens to humans. They come to Earth and get battered, banged around, burned and pounded. That's how the soul grows. As a result of these realizations of the fourth Nafs, there is an increased acceptance that it's all just as it should be, even if it hurts. Even though we don't understand it, it must be the way the Cosmos wants it. There's a growing acceptance of everything, the whole catastrophe.

In the course of developing, we move into the fifth Nafs. Again, there is an incremental jump in consciousness and experience of well-being, as self-absorption is left behind, wonder is increased, and Sa'ada is increased. There is a growing experience of being in contact with Being, with all of the resulting gifts that pour upon us. The Sufis call this 'Baraka,' or grace. We begin to realize that grace is pouring upon us every minute that we are alive on the Earth.

There is an increasing awareness in the fifth Nafs of the miraculousness of life. As we move from Nafs to Nafs, we experience experiential shifts. The soul is being refined and sensitized, so that it is becoming more capable of experiencing the qualities of Being. It has more capacity for inner experience. There is literally more experience available to us. With the fifth Nafs, we have the beginning of the realization of our unity with Being. This is the experience for which Hallaj, a Sufi mystic, was crucified. He said publicly, "I am God." The people in the Islamic community around him thought this was heresy. They did not understand that he was having a mystical experience. He was, in fact, having the experience of the fifth Nafs, the experience of realizing that he was actually the Cosmos in human form. This is the same experience to which the Hindus referred 3,500 years ago. They got it down on paper in the Upanishads. It is the realization that we are the Cosmos forming Itself into this particular human form at this particular moment. It is the same realization that is occurring right now in quantum physics. Quantum physics is now saying that all of creation is a singularity, a unified field with no separate parts. From the Big Bang until now, over 13.7 billion years, there has been only one thing here. That one thing has the miraculous capacity to throw up a material Cosmos of forms that includes us and everything around us. Beneath this material world of forms, there is a silent, still, fertile, living, conscious Field that is throwing up the material realm and metamorphosing it, second by second. That invisible Livingness is the Cosmos. Livingness is not just a phenomenon residing in the Cosmos. It is the primal and primordial nature of the Cosmos Itself. The Cosmos is the primordial principle of Livingness. It is the primordial principle of Consciousness. We are engaged in miracle here. Whether or not we're totally asleep to it, we're engaged in miracle every second that we are awake, alive and conscious on the Earth.

The fifth Nafs is the beginning of the 'Journey *as* Being.' This is equivalent to the realization that we (and everything else) are the Cosmos. There are three journeys involved in the unfolding of the Nafs. The first is the 'Journey *to* Being,' finding our way from an alienated, cut-off, isolated human being to awareness of invisible Being. Being has nothing for the senses to hook into. We have to somehow develop a sensitivity with the cells of our body to feel it somatically, in the space around us. We have to learn to feel through the surface of the world into the Living Nothingness that is beneath and throwing up the forms of the material realm. We can see only the material world, which is just the top layer, the crust of reality. Beneath the material layer is a cosmic Ocean of pure Potential, pure Consciousness, pure Livingness. It's dynamic. It's the power that blows the tops off of volcanoes, blows stars apart, makes planets swirl and galaxies collide. It's magnificent. The 'Journey *to* Being" is the process of finding Being, becoming able to touch Its magnificence. The 'Journey *to* Being' is the process involved in Nafs one, two and three.

The second journey is the 'Journey *with* Being.' This is basically the process involved in the fourth Nafs, the Serene Nafs. At this point, we are conscious of Being and having continuous experience of It. We are living with It, not as an experience that we have once a month for 5 seconds, but an experience that we have every day. We are beginning to be able to perceive Being unfolding Itself as the material world, dynamically throwing it up and constantly metamorphosing and changing it. We are living with that realization. This is the essence of the 'Journey *with* Being.'

The final journey is the 'Journey *as* Being.' This occurs in Nafs five, six and seven. In the very highly developed consciousness of these Nafs, one is constantly aware that one is the Cosmos. It is an expanding awareness. At the beginning, it comes in a very slight form. By the time we get to the seventh Nafs, we are functioning all the time as the Cosmos in a human body for the short period of our time on Earth.

In the sixth Nafs, service to other people and to Being Itself becomes primary. There is almost no ego left at this point. We are no longer interested in achievement or accolade for ourselves. The center of concern is to throw our energies and whatever capacities we have into the world, in order to push humanity forward into contact with Being. The person in the sixth Nafs radiates a positive energy field. In their presence, it is palpable. They have a highly developed sense of Macro-reality. They are no longer interested in details. They are focussed on the Cosmos and Macro-reality. The details of human life are pretty much irrelevant, not important enough to deal with. The pursuit of truth has become primary. Nothing stands in their way of finding the truth of Reality. Service is also primary. Teaching and healing are common pursuits in the sixth Nafs. This person makes a real difference in the lives of other people. They are filled with and radiating a positive energy, which, in fact, is not their own energy. It is the energy of the Cosmos channeling through their organism and spreading Itself in patterns of influence. They have become part of the unfolding cosmic process. They have become, in fact, the expression of the end result of the process, where the whole process has been headed all along. They are having a positive experience of the Cosmos that is so powerful that it tends to spread everywhere. It has become contagious. The people that it spreads to also spread it, and those people spread it further. There is a ripple effect. The truth of the Cosmos, the deep nature of the Cosmos, is revealing Itself in spreading waves through humankind.

The person in the sixth Nafs is full of wonder. They are in bliss much of the time. They do not have their feet on the ground any longer. Their connection to everyday life has become tenuous. We can't have everything at once. We are not going to find someone who is highly financially responsible in the sixth Nafs. They simply don't have time for it. Their attention is elsewhere, focussed on more important matters.

By the sixth Nafs, the energy in the psychic system has moved from the head to the heart. One has become primarily a channel for heart experience. We have many reports of such highly developed people in India. The United States may not be an environment that is conducive to nurture these individuals. They are likely to be misunderstood and marginalized.

The person in the sixth Nafs may not be entirely capable of fending for themselves. They may need an organization around them to take care of them. They can get lost in bliss, which is their path and their function in life. They are on Earth to demonstrate this possibility. They are filled with a sense of the Sublime, an on-going opening of the heart to the miraculous quality of the Cosmos. They are blissed out, and humanity is the better for it.

The seventh Nafs is Perfection, the Perfect Human, evidencing union with Being. The ego has disappeared. Sa'ada is permanent. The burgeoning qualities and experiences of the previous Nafs come to complete fruition. A sense of wonder and the miraculous are sustained and permanent. The perspective on life shifts to the standpoint of the Cosmos rather than the human viewpoint. The human in the seventh Nafs radiates warmth, benevolence, compassion and tenderness. He or she accepts that the Cosmos is unfolding Its plan perfectly, though we may not be able to understand it. So, the person in the seventh Nafs will not be overly concerned with death, injustice or social causes.

If it is unfolding, it must be according to the plan of the Cosmos. Obviously, few humans reach this final stage of development, perhaps less than a handful in centuries. After the seventh Nafs, there remains only 'Fana,' (extinction), total absorption back into the Sea of Being.

15
Images and Symbols

Sometimes,
when the light
is right,
I see through the crust of the world.
I'm enveloped
in moments of wonder,
in the richness
of Living Light,
and I touch
the deep realities
that lie just beyond my sight.
My heart fills up
and I can see
the Life that stretches
in every direction
and reaches into infinity.

Our life is laced with images. They are the basic unit of consciousness. Images were the first language of humankind, in place and driving our survival millennia before we learned to speak. Imagery probably produced language, arising from the grunts and gestures of semi-apes trying earnestly to communicate what they were experiencing in their head. Today, images are still the language of the unconscious mind and the language of the soul. All day and all night, images flow through our minds like pearls on a string, each entering, floating through and exiting, to be succeeded by the next. They are the continuous thread of our consciousness.

Imagery is not highly regarded in our culture. Perhaps because our lives are awash with images, from magazines, newspapers, movies, television, the web, advertisements and ten thousand other sources, we do not usually consider them to be very important. The exception, of course, is the advertising industry, which carefully uses imagery in order to sell us things. Generally, however, we do not consider images to be crucial. We fail to realize that they can be dynamic. They can make things happen. We generally do not distinguish between junk images, from mass media and pop culture, that contain nothing of importance, and significant, important images that could potentially change our lives.

Carl Jung did the deepest, best work on images and symbols. His students and successors have added much good information to elaborate what he started. Jungian therapy today is primarily a study of the client's imagery, from dreams and waking visions, hopefully emerging from the unconscious level. Jung was vitally interested in the deep, usually symbolic imagery carried in the human unconscious. This imagery formulates our perceptions, interpretations and responses to life, tracks the arc of our life as we move through it, and is the source of the shifting, changing transformations that we experience.

A symbol is a very special kind of image. Image is the generic term, but when we say symbol we mean something very specific. A symbol must be distinguished from a sign. A sign is a basic equivalence. A stands for B. You know what A is and you know what B is. An example is the cross, which stands for Christianity. There is no mystery in the meaning. It's just a simple equivalence. When you see the cross you know you're talking Christianity. Signs are totally within the framework of consciousness and rationality.

A symbol, on the other hand, comes from beneath the threshold of the conscious mind. It comes wrapped in mystery. We cannot see where it comes from, and we probably will not know what it means. It comes laden with meaning. Sometimes it comes with multiple meanings, all of which may be simultaneously true. The symbol is a vein of richness in consciousness. If we can tap into that vein, we can learn things that we need to know. The symbol points beyond itself. It points beyond what is known or knowable. It reaches down into regions of vastness, infinity and mystery. It relates to the human search for significance and meaning. Symbols don't create meaning in the mind. They simply open meaning in consciousness. Symbols very often relate to the sense of sacredness, the sense of majesty in the universe. The Sufi definition of sacredness is: "Meaningfulness perceived with the heart."

Symbols cannot be constructed. They cannot be forced. They must be approached on their own terms. They simply arrive. They are an act of grace, a gift of information. They are not rational. They arise out of the darkness of the depths. But, they can be crucial to our lives. All we can do with symbols is wait expectantly, and catch them if they arrive. Man has been called "the Symbolic Animal." Eli Sagan said: "A human need is powerful as sex or aggression, a need that can be denied the psyche only at the cost of severe psychic disorder, is the need to create symbols and live in a symbolic world."

Symbols are numinous, or lit up. They are mysterious and compelling to the human personality. Although we may not know what they mean, they compel and constellate our attention. They are magnetic, attracting our attention and curiosity. We sense something deep and rich in them, and we are eager to excavate it. Symbols arrive with the conviction that there is something extraordinary here, something that is veiled, true and can only partially be seen. And, as their influence deepens, they can become very dynamic and cause human behavior to change. They can occasionally become a molder and moving force in consciousness.

One cannot talk intelligently about images and symbols without mentioning the Mithal. The Mithal is one of the great ideas of Ibn Arabi, (12ᵗʰ century Arab Spain). Ibn Arabi postulated that between the level of invisible, absolute Being and the level of the material world is an in-between realm that he called the Mithal, that is totally image. The images in this realm have their own reality and manner of working, their own idiosyncratic dynamics, which is totally unlike that of the material world. However, the images penetrate our world and our consciousness. They play a large and vital part in our lives. They appear in our consciousness with potentially powerful effects.

Because the Mithal is an interface, an in-between zone, the material world can leak up into it and become a little spiritualized. When that happens, we call it idealization. Pure Being, which is unseeable, can leak down into the Mithal, enabling us to have images of spiritual realities that cannot be seen otherwise. Examples are the images of Shiva dancing his eternal dance of destruction, and God touching the finger of Adam on the ceiling of the Sistine Chapel. These spiritualized visions have become the basis for all the world's great religions. The Mithal is a mysterious, in-between realm, with some access to Being and some access to the material world, both realms leaking into it. The imagery that floats through our minds every day is emerging from the Mithal. It comes, perhaps, through the filter of our own personality and our own world view, but the imagery itself comes from the Mithal.

Science, of course, would sneer at this idea but, as a matter of fact, Einstein expertly used images to arrive at his conclusions. He called them "thought experiments."

For his part, Carl Jung credited many of his ideas to Philamon, a Pagan old man with a beard and wings, who existed in Jung's imagination. At a certain stage in his life, Jung spent a great deal of time talking in his mind with Philamon. He later said "I owe my career to Philamon." There is something strange at work here, quite outside our worldview. Jung is conversing with an image in his mind, getting information that he didn't have before, that proved crucial to the development of his ideas.

A very similar process was reported by Ibn Arabi. He described how he imagined himself walking around and around the Ka'aba in Mecca with Sophia, the Goddess of Wisdom. She was in the guise of a young girl. As they circumnavigated the Ka'aba in his mind, they talked at length. Like Jung, Ibn Arabi credited this imaginal friend as the source of many of his most important ideas.

These examples show that we should not be derisive about the imagination. The imagination is a powerful tool for determining reality, particularly if the subject matter is too vast or too small to be seen with the eyes. If something is invisible but real, how else would we perceive it? Imagination, in some circumstances, can be a source of truth about reality. Here's what Maria Von Franz, the foremost pupil of Jung, said about imagery: "A dream, (image) comments on the person's situation. It can vivify something which is happening in a person's life. It gives a sense of the problem as having a hidden meaning even though the meaning may not be clear. The knowledge from the unconscious is the water of life. Having drunk of it, the person will feel that something is flowing and the period of stagnation is over. Working in this way is the uniting of the conscious with the unconscious."

This is a testament by a brilliant mind to the power of imagery. We need access to our deep imagery in order to live our lives fully. We need our dreaming sight in order to be whole. Henry Corbin said: "Once we lost sight of the imaginal nature of certain realities, the true import of a great body of mythic and religious teachings slipped from our grasp." Reality is so much richer and more complex than we imagine it to be. Images and symbols are a central feature of that rich layering. They are gifts to us of in-depth meaning. At this stage in our evolution, we know very little about where they come from, or how, but we can say with conviction that they are connected to Reality, connected to the depths of our consciousness, our livingness, and to the depths of Being Itself.

16
Synchronicity

From harmonic patterns
in the depths of Being
the things of the Cosmos
come forth.
My consciousness too
is a flowering
of patterns held in the fullness of space.
Mind and matter are coming
from the same invisible place.
Thrown up by the power
of unseeable Force,
reality emerges
from the Living Source.

Synchronicity is a term that was coined by Jung. He noticed in his therapy practice that often strange coincidences would happen in the lives of his clients. Things would come up simultaneously in the mind and in the material world. This was striking because, in the consensus reality, there is no way that the two can be connected. It was a complete anomaly, but it happened again and again. He became interested in this phenomenon of coincidental happenings. He called them "acausal orderedness." The word acausal means outside of cause-and-effect. His full definition was "the coincidence in time of two or more causally unrelated events which have the same meaning." One thing that his definition did not do is point out that the two events occur in different realms. One of them manifests in consciousness and the other manifests in the material world. Their interrelationship is unquestionable and a little erie.

Two examples that Jung gave show this relationship of mind and matter. He was walking with a client in the park. The client was relating a dream that she had just had that involved coming down a stairway in the ancestral home. In the dream, a fox came down the stairway with her at the same time. As she was relating the dream, a fox came out of the forest and walked in front of Jung and his client for a long time. Both Jung and the client were startled by the coincidence.

The second event took place in Jung's office. He was having a session with a very difficult, hyper-rational client. He was having difficulty getting her to break through the prison of her excessive rationality. She was telling him about a dream she had had the night before about an Egyptian scarab beetle, which Jung knew was a symbol of rebirth. Just at that moment, a rustling at the window attracted Jung's attention. He went over and opened it and there was a scarab beetle. Jung grasped it, took it over to the client, and said: "Here is your scarab beetle." The coincidence broke through her rationality and allowed her to make great progress afterward.

Although the incidents that he related were anecdotal and appeared to be trivial, he knew very well that there was something mysterious and important involved. He was quite aware that he was opening the question of whether there is a part of reality that we do not understand, that is beyond cause and effect. That question was also the source of the fascination that Jung felt with the I Ching. The I Ching, of course, is a Chinese system of divination where you throw yarrow sticks or coins six times. The results are translated into a patterned hexagram, which is then interpreted by reference to a manuscript of cryptic sayings. Anybody who's ever thrown the I Ching knows that it is strangely, startlingly accurate. It can answer questions. It is based on the ancient Chinese supposition that the universe is permeated with a vast hidden order in which all things are connected. The I Ching is considered a doorway into the hidden order that lies beneath reality. Today we would call this hidden order 'Patterns of Being,' held in the invisible realm of Being, that occasionally emerge into the material world as an orchestrated reality.

Jung had a much broader mind than we ordinarily credit him with having. He was in touch with the quantum physicists of his day, who were discovering a number of startling things about the nature of reality. Their discoveries were, in fact, cutting the legs out from under what we have believed about reality for the last 400 years. Jung knew the men doing this transformative research. He had many long conversations over dinner with Einstein. He was intimately acquainted with the work of Niels Bohr and Wolfgang Pauli was actually a therapy client of Jung's.

Jung was quite aware that the very basis of reality was being questioned, that the way that we have understood reality for the past 400 years is reductionist and too small. Jung knew that. His work with synchronicity was, in fact, pressing toward the same ultimate questions about reality. Unfortunately, he died before he could apply his full genius to that question.

The quantum physicists of his day were realizing that, if you follow the material realm down to the smallest levels, it disappears into space and energy. The electrons that circle the nucleus of an atom jump from orbit to orbit without passing in between. This is not the world of Newton and Descartes. This is not the orderly world of dead and empty space, with solid forms drifting through it and colliding like billiard balls. The billiard ball universe is simply too small as an explanation of reality. Jung could see the similarities between what he was observing psychologically in his clients, and what was emerging in quantum physics.

Today, about 70 years later, this line of inquiry around synchronicity is under study as the new thought on Macro-reality. Avant-garde science is looking specifically at the connection between mind and matter. How are these two realms interlaced with each other and part of, perhaps, one reality instead of two realities? We are realizing that the two may arise from the same source. They may be connected in ways that we have not even suspected.

The dying worldview, which is still the consensus view, is the legacy of Descartes. Descartes divided mind and matter into two separate camps and said, basically, that we cannot study mind. There is nothing there to experiment with. We must set mind aside and not worry with it. We must deal exclusively with matter. The culture took him at his word, and, for the past 400 years, we have scarcely investigated consciousness. With matter, experimental results can be retested, and confirmed or contradicted. Empirical experiments are possible. With invisible consciousness, this is not the case. Unfortunately, the materialist approach left consciousness totally outside investigation. Today, scientists cannot tell us what consciousness is. Their best guess, and it is not a very good one, is that consciousness is an epiphenomenon, or byproduct, of the brain. They are now engaged, successfully, in mapping the brain to determine which portions of the brain are linked with which experiences in human consciousness. This approach does not address the phenomenon of consciousness. It addresses only the phenomenon of the brain, which may be only a filter of consciousness. It is based on the assumption that matter produces consciousness, that the brain produces awareness and consciousness. The truth is exactly the opposite. It is consciousness that is the primary phenomenon in the universe. Consciousness produces matter, the material world. The scientists have got it exactly backwards. They are unable with their framework to answer questions about a whole raft of things such as telepathy and distant vision, that have been documented over and over. This is where we have been for the last 400 years. We are still there.

Now, however, there is a whole group of people who are beginning to suspect that, in fact, consciousness and the material realm share the same source. The same sense of interiority that we experience in our human consciousness is in the Cosmos. Everything has interiority, or consciousness. We are talking here about a conscious Universe. In order to accept that, the scientific establishment would have to throw out the Universe that was constructed from the visions of Newton and Descartes, the visions of a dead and empty universe. A dead and empty cosmos is not a fit Universe to live in. It reduces human life to absolute futility. It means that there is nothing sublime and grand and mysterious and Cosmic and alive. There is nothing, of which we are a single tiny part that is absolutely miraculous and wondrous. It's all just dead, empty space. We are among among the very few little pieces of the world that are conscious and alive. Most of it is dead and empty. We cannot live in a dead and empty Cosmos and feel great about it. It will leave us in despair and desolation. It is will leave us alienated and separate. It will leave us with an absolute sense of futility and a terrible sadness about our life, because we are not part of anything that's deep, sacred, meaningful and miraculous.

We have come to the place in human evolution where we must grow past the worldview of a dead and empty cosmos. It has now become destructive of our life and our mental health. The Cosmos is conscious throughout. Everything we see is built of Consciousness. There is nothing outside the Sea of Consciousness. What we see in the material world are forms that are a temporary aggregation of quantum particles, pulling themselves together into forms that are temporary. After a certain length of time, those particles will separate and recycle themselves into other forms. We can see that the forms in our world are transitory. They are brought together as quantum particles to become forms. They come apart after a time, and go back into the Sea of particles. And, the particles are alive. The Universe is a Sea of Livingness, constantly throwing up the material realm and recycling it into other forms. This is the eternal way the Cosmos unfolds.

This leads to the corollary that the consciousness that we are experiencing inside our heads is the same consciousness that exists throughout the Universe. We have access to a little pool of this miracle for a limited time. The brain, in this viewpoint, does not produce consciousness. It filters it into the human. It is the interface with the vast consciousness of the Universe. The brain is taking the consciousness of the Universe and transforming it into what we experience as our personal consciousness.

The Universe is conscious as a totality. The idea that it is a vast Sea of Consciousness is consistent with the idea in quantum physics that the universe is a unified field. If the Cosmos is wholly connected at the material level, and it is only one thing, without separate parts of any kind, why would it not be connected at the level of consciousness as well? The primordial patterns and unity of Being are inherent in immaterial consciousness just as they are in the material realm.

We are growing into the realization that we are the Cosmos. We are in a human form, walking the earth for a short time, as the cutting edge of Cosmic evolution. The latest thing that is happening, and it is very exciting, is that we are realizing our new and true identity. Our consciousness has now evolved to the point where we can look at ourselves and realize that we are the Cosmos. We are the Cosmos regarding the Cosmos, experiencing Itself. We are the vehicles through which that is happening. Quantum physics opened the door and offered us the opportunity to rethink our conclusions about the nature of reality. Now we have reached the point where we can redefine the human being. Our new definition is: 'We are the Cosmos.' Our ideas of who and what we are are changing and our concepts of Macro-reality are changing. We are in full flux now.

17
Omnicentrism

Everywhere is the center
of the conscious, mysterious Sea.
The Field is living throughout.
New life can emerge,
without a doubt,
at every single point.
Our consciousness too
is a center of life,
a marvelous, focused store
of coherence,
and perception,
and integration,
and sublime Being, and more.
We fit perfectly into the world.
We are at its very core.

One of the strange aspects of reality is that the center of the Universe is everywhere. It's a little hard to get our mind around this. The Universe is omnicentric. Omni means everywhere. The center of the Cosmos is everywhere. This is a consequence of the fact that the Universe is a single, living Field of Being. Every point in the Field is fertile, vital and living. The Universe can create a new center or new system of life at any point within Itself. That's the nature of a Field. Every point in the Field shares the same characteristics. In the case of the Cosmos, those characteristics are generativity, livingness and consciousness.

We can observe this fertility all around us. The power of the Universe to create new centers of life is everywhere. It is continually forming new centers that are highly organized and effectively integrated systems of distinct, new, individual organisms. They have autonomy. They have identifiable, separate sets of characteristics. Examples are hummingbirds, beetles, and elephants. Each of these is an autonomous center of life or system of life.

As we look back into the past, we see that species have evolved and metamorphosed. Fish came out of the ocean as the Lungfish and turned into mammals on land. That was the creation of a new, living center in the Cosmos. Evolution keeps moving from one center to another, yielding an ever-increasing complexity of the Universe. Another example of a new center was the development of single cells in the ocean 4 billion years ago. There was no life in those waters, then suddenly a living cell emerged. That cell developed a membrane around it, allowing it to survive. It was quite a feat to invent a membrane that protected it from the environment and allowed its life to continue.

Of course, our interest here is humans. Each human being on Earth is the center of the Universe. This is the way of the Universe. What does it mean to be a center of the Universe, to be a system of life, to be central to reality? Here is what the Hindus said about it:

"I am a center. Around me revolves my world. I am a center of influence. I am a center of consciousness. I am a center of thought. I am a center of information. I am a center of vitality. I am a center of force. I am a center of energy. I am a center of dynamic will, I make things happen. I am a center of strength. I am a center of power. I am a center of knowledge. I am a center of mind. I am a center of being. I am a center of spirit. I am a center of soul. I am a center of the universe. I claim my birth right."

Each human being is both a unique system of life, thrown up from the depths of living Being, and an indivisible part of the Cosmos as a singular thing, a unified Field. The Cosmos has unfolded over 13.7 billion years, but it's a single thing. There are no separate parts in the universe, but there are concentrations of life, or centers, throughout the universe.

The full range of the universe's capabilities is available at every point in the Field of the Cosmos. It is obvious that the universe must create or fit the new center, if it is to flourish, into conditions that will allow it to sustain its life, but it has a wonderful talent for generating new systems of life anywhere that it chooses to do so. An example is the organisms that live on hot vents at the bottom of the ocean. These living organisms are living in enormous temperatures. The magma at the core of the earth is pouring boiling water and steam up into the ocean. These organisms live right in the middle of that boiling water, right at the vent down into the magma. They also live under enormous pressure, thousands of feet under the surface of the ocean, with the weight of all that water on them. They live in total darkness. Scientists were amazed when they found these creatures living in such conditions. It was startling to realize that life was possible in such extreme conditions.There is a new discipline emerging these days called Astrobiology. This discipline is organized around searching for life on other planets, but it is also raising new questions about what constitutes life and what conditions can sustain life. The answers are much broader than we thought. Life is perhaps not limited to carbon based organisms that we see around us. Instead of being carbon based, perhaps life can be based on methane or other gas, or acid-based or arsenic-based. These are questions that never occurred to us before, but what we're seeing in the scientific investigation that is going on in Astrobiology is that life may be much broader than we thought. All the questions relating to life must be rethought.

What we're talking about here are aspects of the creativity of the Universe. We are looking at the mechanics of the creativity of the Universe. How is it that the Universe has an unfathomable creativity at every point in the Cosmos? How does it continually bring together disparate parts and create these entirely new systems that are self sustaining and capable of reproducing themselves? Each of these systems, a hummingbird, an elephant, is a center of life, a center of the Universe and a focus of the incredible creative power that is spilling forth from unexpressed potential. It continues to do so today in our own lives. Evolution or metamorphosis usually happens too slowly for us to watch it happen. We can only look backwards and see this cornucopia of life flowing forth, but the process is on-going. It is an inherent characteristic of the Cosmos.

Evolution and creation continue all around us. Each of these new centers of life, when it's created, has to have an environment that's compatible. It doesn't exist in isolation. It has to be seamlessly woven into what already exists. The universe does that and correlates everything together. We can observe an incredible diversity and multiplicity of life forms all interwoven with each other and all perfectly correlated together so that they fill each other's needs. It's truly an ecosystem on a cosmic scale.

Living systems have to have access to food sources in order to obtain energy, but the kinds of things that they can eat are almost infinite. The world that we live in depends on photosynthesis. At some point in the evolution of life on Earth, a developing cellular organism, which was later going to be a plant, developed the capacity to grab sunlight. It developed a molecule that could turn sunlight into energy, so that it could live on that energy. That also is almost beyond our capacity to grasp. The intelligence that could enable a plant to grab sunlight and make energy for its own use is mind-boggling. Subsequently, plants spread across the Earth, each with this remarkable capability. The plant-life on Earth, and indeed all life on Earth, was made possible by this ability of plants to capture sunlight and turn it into energy for their growth and reproduction. Then, of course, the mammals ate the plants and each other. So sunlight and the process of photosynthesis are supporting all life on Earth.

The layers of life are stacked on top of each other. Each of them must solve the problems of finding a food source, reproducing and fitting into the ongoing environment. If the organism does not solve these problems adequately, it ceases to exist as a center. It disappears. The universe appears to proceed by trial and error. If the organisms that it generates do not seamlessly fit into the existing systems of life, they are terminated.

The human ego, which we experience every minute of every day, is an example of a coherent, workable and integrated system or center created by the Universe. We experience our consciousness as a wholeness. It is a seamless center of awareness that allows us to perceive the world and respond to it. We know that not so long ago this miraculous consciousness originated as simple animal consciousness, something much more basic, the mind of an ape. As the Cosmos unfolded those apes, they became us.

We are observing ceaseless evolution and creation of new centers of life. We are watching as this immensely creative and efficient system unfolds Itself. From what or from where? It is unfolding these living centers from Livingness that is invisible, beneath the material world. It unfolds a center of material life and we call it an animal, an organism, but the genesis of that life is the unseen. It is coming from the level of Being that we can never see. There is nothing at that level but pure Livingness, nothing for our senses to hook into. It is pure, generative potential.

The Universe is able to organize these centers of life into impossibly intricate organisms, such as ourselves. When the organization of the organisms is upset, or is not quite right, we can have something like autism resulting. The correlation of all the processes that make up human consciousness don't work exactly right. The person is caught in a realm outside of normal functionality. They are not able to perceive the world and have a response to it that makes a human life effective and fruitful.

The Universe apparently makes mistakes and then weeds out the mistakes. What's left to take forward are the successes. It builds on Its own successes over billions of years. We are miracles walking. It takes a trillion interactions per second to keep each of us on the Earth. There are a trillion cells in the body. Every single one of those cells is making its contribution to the organism as a whole. We are more like a coral reef than anything else, a collection of a trillion cellular entities all cooperating and interacting to make our organism function. To go to a deeper level, we are a collection of a practically infinite number of particles, electrons swirling around a nucleus. The net result is that we are here, on the Earth's surface for a short period of time, as a coherent, integrated being that can walk and talk and have a life. Our true nature at a deeper level is collegiate, in the sense that it's multiple. We are, in fact, a large colony of multiple organisms organized perfectly into a whole for the sake of functionality.

Each of us, as a center of the Universe, has a unique perspective on the world. We are each a center of the universe, looking out into our world. We call the experience of this perspective the Self, but we could as well call it the Center. This centeredness is not just a viewpoint. It's our basic reality. The universe has given each of us a totally unique and totally individual window onto reality. We are truly a center of the universe, and from that center we look out into our unique, individual reality. Every single one of us, in our own way and through our own lens, has our own singular perceptions. We put them together in an individual way, and we come up with interpretations that are totally our own. Nobody else puts life together quite like we do. It's a very individual and very unique thing.

Human relationships would go a lot smoother if we kept this in mind. The person that we are dealing with is a separate, little universe. They may look generic, but they are nothing like us. They have nothing of our personal history. They have nothing of the way that we have organized our perceptions into a coherent whole so that we can navigate the world. They are probably not arriving at the same conclusions as we are about life and reality in general. If we understood that, perhaps we would not be appalled or angry when someone sees something differently than we do, when they act in a way that we would not act. Perhaps we might, instead, be curious about how the world looks from inside their totally unique reality. Perhaps we might consciously remember that they are also a center of the universe, a center with its own integrity and its own coherence. Human relationships might be quite different if we operated from this basis.

It is possible that we are now experiencing a leap in evolution, a hyper-evolution. There is something going on at present that is bringing a new level of awareness of ourselves as the Cosmos. In fact, if this is happening, as it appears to be, this would be the establishment of a new center of consciousness by the Cosmos. We are moving into something new, something not seen before. Our consciousness is shifting and moving into an expanded space. The universe is unfolding us. It is unfolding and expanding our consciousness.

Out of Its pure potential, It is changing the human being and making us into something new and different. Part of this is observable in quantum physics. In the past few decades, probably the last 70 years, we have realized that the reality system that we have been living with is not adequate. The framework that was formulated by Isaac Newton and Rene Descartes is characterized by a dead and empty cosmos, functioning mechanically like a clock. That worldview is breaking down. It is no longer adequate as a framework for human life. We are now realizing, from all of the information of quantum physics that we now have about particles and their entanglement with each other, that cause and effect is not the only process operating in the universe. We know about the Field Itself, and Its marvelous properties. We know that Macro-reality is a singular Unified Field. Everything that we experience is occurring within the Field. We are becoming aware of that.

We are in a phase where our very definition of ourselves is changing. We are realizing that we are not, in fact, separate entities walking on the Earth. We are, instead, integral parts of a single, vast organism, the Cosmos, that is unfolding Itself and revealing Its new possibilities. That is rapidly becoming our definition of ourselves. We are realizing that we are the Cosmos Itself, temporarily in human form for a short span of time. In due time, our forms will disappear back into the sea of Being. Other humans will come and have their time on Earth. The fact is that we now know that the Cosmos has been a single, living entity for the last 13.7 billion years. It has had its phases as galaxies, and as exploding stars which blew carbon to the earth. That carbon became us through a long process of single cells in the oceans becoming fish, which invented spines, eyes, sexual organs, digestive systems, and other wondrous necessities of life. They were very talented fish. They eventually came out on to the land and became mammals, the mammals became apes and the apes became us. It is an astonishing, mind-boggling scenario.

These are some of our new realizations. Our definition of ourselves is expanding, broadening, and changing radically. If we are given time to grow into these new ideas, it will yield a new world and a new Cosmos. It can't come a moment too soon.

18
The Realm of Archetypes

The Cosmos has an interior,
invisible, living, aware,
filled with the blueprints
of Cosmic life
and bursting with potential.
Our minds have an interior too,
invisible, living, aware,
filled with the blueprints
of Cosmic life
and bursting with potential.
It's one and the same,
whatever its name,
these unseen patterns of life.
We can see the world
but can never see
its Source,
the living Interiority.

We owe our modern understanding of archetypes to Carl Jung. Jung, in speculating about archetypes, credited Plato with originating the idea. We don't know how much further back in history the idea might have existed before Plato. Plato's concept was that, in an invisible realm, there are ideal forms existing that form the patterns for the objects that we encounter in the material world. A table that exists in the material world, for instance, is a counterpart to an ideal table in the realm of pure idea. In his view, all material tables emerge through the pattern of that pure concept, the ideal but invisible table. As between the two realms, Plato said that the ideal realm is the more important realm, because everything around us in the material realm is going to erode and disappear, but the ideal realm is unchanging and eternal. Plato put the realm of his ideal forms above the material realm.

Jung took this idea, modified it and applied it to human beings. He postulated that humans carry images deeply buried in their unconsciousness that mold them, mold their lives and mold each generation of new humans as they come onto the earth. In Jung's system, an archetype is a blueprint for how to live a human life.

It actually is, in a certain sense, a map of the Journey of the Soul. The idea is that, at each phase of life, a different archetype is expressed through the structure of the Deep Mind. An archetype informs a baby how to be a baby. When the person becomes a child, another archetype tells the organism how to be a little child. As it becomes a teenager, another archetype appears, with instructions to follow. The young adult has his/her archetypal instructions, and when they become a mother or father, the archetype is there with its knowledge. The patterns of this unfolding line of archetypes continue until the end of life. Viewed as the Journey of the Soul, one moves serially from archetype to archetype as one progresses through the arc of one's life. The archetype that is presently constellating for us is telling us who and what to be. It is determining our orientation, our wants and our behavior. It is the patterning in the process of being human. We cannot operate outside of its patterns. Archetypes are omnipresent, found everywhere and in every person, because the themes of human life are constant.

The number of patterns that we can call upon to act human are limited. In the world, we can observe the King archetype operating in every CEO. It involves controlling from the top of a hierarchy, using this position of supremacy to inform the people lower down the ladder how things are going to be. The King exercises power over others. The King archetype silently instructs the CEO how to be a King, how to act as the person at the top of the hierarchy.

If we look toward sports, we will see the Hero archetype emerging. People are out there, doing battle, on the football field or basketball or hockey court, or whatever. They are straining every nerve to be the Hero, to be the one that makes the winning score, that gets the glory, that receives the accolades (read olive branch). The competing teams are enacting a prototype of battle, of war. The members are individually expressing the Hero archetype. They are caught up in the Hero archetype. It is fueling their behavior and experience. They are chasing it. It propelled them into the game in the first place. In playing it out, they are chasing the rewards of the archetype.

Jung succinctly said, "An archetype is a living organism endowed with generative force." The keyword here is living. Jung's concept was not that of some kind of a dead pattern, but a living, generative force which influences and shapes human beings and their behavior. A longer definition that he gave us is, "An active, living disposition with the capacity to initiate, control and mediate human behavior." For 'disposition' we could substitute 'deep structure.'

We are in the presence of something very mysterious here. The patterns that are invisibly held in the psyche are in the very structure of our consciousness. They are controlling our life. They are providing the pathways through which our life is flowing. Jung considered these archetypes to be held in the Collective Unconscious. That concept, the Collective Unconscious, is becoming very important right now. The concept of a Collective Unconscious lifts us out of the box of the idea that consciousness is located only inside our head, inside the human brain.

The Collective Unconscious is a Field of Consciousness that is shared by all humanity. It is a part of us all. It is becoming important to the new thought because it provides a model for consciousness held in the Field outside of human beings. The avant-garde thinkers are leaving behind the Newtonian/ Cartesian reality system that insists that the Universe is dead and empty. The new thought says that it is a Universe full of Consciousness, Awareness and Life. Jung's concept of the Collective Unconscious laid a bridge for these thinkers to assert that we're in a vast field of Consciousness residing outside of the human brain.

Jung held that the Collective Unconscious contains all of the experiences of human history. The experience of every human who ever lived is held in the Collective Unconscious. The archetypes that reside in the Collective Unconscious carry images, but they are much more than just roles or images. They are dynamic energies that are manifesting in human lives. They determine our perceptions and our behavior from the depths of the most basic structure of our consciousness.

The archetypes are very close in nature to myths. Both contain the basic themes that are embodied in human life, the themes that humans live out generation after generation, themes such as the Wise Old Man, the Great Mother, the Trickster, the Hero, etc. When a baby is born to a woman, the Mother archetype emerges to assist the new mother. She may need a little help with the details, but she knows in her basic being how to mother the child. The information is encoded into her deepest nature, into her being itself, at the deepest levels of her being. It is instinct. The mothering instinct comes forth and she does what is necessary to keep that baby alive. The archetype is thus engaged with the continuance of the species. It tells us how to survive and continue ourselves.

Every human life is the enactment of a drama. This drama can be viewed through the eyes of myth, or it can be viewed through the eyes of the archetypes. The archetypes are the Journey of the Soul in a deep way. They are waiting as scripts to carry us through the process of being human and having a human life while we're on Earth. The archetypes are the matrix of our life experience. They are the ground from which our individual personality or ego emerges. We are very aware of our separateness, but we are not aware of the deep level at which we are all connected. We are all one thing. You might call it humanity. You might call it centers of being. We come from a deep common ground. Our instinctual energy is channeled through the archetypes, which instruct us how to be human.

We are patterned creatures. The deep patterns are always active in whatever phase we happen to be in in our lives. Jung called archetypes 'Primordial Images,' primordial connoting that there is nothing deeper than this. The operation of the images in our psyche produces our self-image, structures how we think about ourselves, and how we identify ourselves. It produces our decisions. It prompts us to act. It produces our behavior. We're very close here to the operations of the mythical Greek gods. The Greeks understood their gods as energies, as impulses that descended into the human realm, manifested, and made things happen in human life. The gods were formative principles responsible for structuring human life, for animating and ordering human life and energizing and ordering experience. Jung called the archetypes 'organizing factors.' His definitions encompass the whole concept of archetypes, but note that we can never see an archetype. We may see the images and perhaps the behavior generated by the archetype, but the archetype themselves are instinctual energies that are swirling in space, alive and dynamic but invisible. These energies, although they themselves cannot be seen, turn themselves into images, which can then be seen in our consciousness.

So we can never see the archetype of Father, because there is nothing there but swirling, inchoate energy. However, in its operation, the Father archetype will turn itself into the image of a male of a certain age who does his part in bringing forth and raising a child. A concept of Father exists which throws up an image. Though it is rooted in the invisible, it can now be seen in the mind's eye. It's an effective way to comprehend archetypes. It takes us to the very deepest levels of consciousness. And, archetypes may go far beyond that.

At the present time, the realization is emerging among the best minds of our generation that the archetypes are much more than just blueprints for human life. They are now investigating whether the archetypes may be as fundamental to cosmology as to psychology. They are speculating that both the Cosmos, in its entirety, and the human psyche emerge from the ground of these patterns. This is an astounding leap, but very important in the unfolding conversation that is changing our reality system. They are saying that the Cosmos and human consciousness may be structured in the same way. This is reminiscent of the ancient Hermetic principle 'As above, so below,' that was put forth thousands of years ago. The Hermetic principles go back to the dawn of time. A related speculation today is that mind and matter are parts of one thing, issuing from the same Source.

This emerging realization involves getting rid of the Newtonian/Cartesian framework. Descartes' idea was that mind and matter are split into two realms. He basically said, "We can't study mind, because there's nothing there for our senses to hook into, so we're just going to set mind aside." As a result, we have not seriously studied consciousness in the past 400 years. We followed Descartes down the wrong path. What we did in the West was study matter exclusively. Our science today is the study of how matter acts and reacts with itself. We are beginning to break out of that box at the present time.

Quantum physics has given us a doorway, a way to break out, by saying that the entire Cosmos is a Unified Field. There are no separate parts. In this thinking, both the Cosmos and the human mind have interiority. Both have consciousness and an interior reality that is completely immaterial. With consciousness, as with Being, there is nothing to grab onto. Our senses cannot perceive consciousness, even in our own minds. When we try to look at our own pool of consciousness, rather than the thoughts that move through it, it is a field of silent, invisible sensitivity. When we try to see it, nothing appears. It is just space, but space that is very talented. It is space that images can move through, thoughts can move through, that concepts can form in. In this space, you can make decisions and manage your life. The space is far from empty. Consciousness is something other. It is an addition to empty space. It is a Livingness that enables us to have our life on Earth. Without consciousness, we cannot have our life. We know almost nothing about this subject. The scientists cannot tell us what Consciousness is. They consider it to be an epiphenomenon, a byproduct of brain function. That has it exactly backwards. The view is based on the idea that matter produces Consciousness. The truth is that Consciousness produces matter. We're at a point now where we are realizing that our old reality system was misguided and incomplete. It had an incorrect view of reality. We are beginning to move to a new worldview, the corollaries of which we cannot see. We have no idea how it will be to live in a world where we realize consciously and continuously that the whole Cosmos is just one thing, changing its shape second to second, instead of separate things bumping around in empty space.

It's an odd time to be alive, because we don't know enough yet to see clearly how life will be in that kind of Cosmos. We can get glimpses of how it might be if we realize that the universe is a singularity, with no parts of any kind. If the universe is a total singularity and all matter is part of that one thing, then all consciousness must be part of that one thing also. There cannot be two categories of anything. There is no place for anything to be harbored and localized. If there is love in a human being, love must exist in the Field. If there is consciousness in a human being, consciousness must exist in the Field. Anything that exists in human life must also exist in the Field, because humans are not separate from the Field in any way. There are no two things. There is only the one thing, the Cosmos, and that is what we are experiencing in our human life. It throws up a whole new universe to perceive this truth. The emerging understanding of archetypes as invisible patterns underlying life will be crucial in this new understanding. Jung said that archetypes must forever remain unknown and mysterious. We can understand bits and pieces about them. We can see images that express them. They are omnipresent in our human life, but we can never get to the bottom of them. They are very mysterious. They cannot be fit into a formula. They are, at bottom, formless, nameless and invisible.

They are the mysterious energy of Being Itself, inherent in the very fabric of reality as a whole. They exist at the level of spirit. A direct encounter with an archetype is an experience of unbridled power, depth and intensity. There is an experience of the numinous (lit-up). There is an experience of mystery, awe, intense religious affect and emotional arousal. Nerves tingle. There is often an experience of overwhelming beauty. Encountering an archetype directly is a spiritual experience of the living Being of the Cosmos.

19
Idealization

The culture is the "World of Lies,"
pandering to the trivial and perverse,
and soaked in self-regard.
Its instructions to us are false.
Leave behind
this realm of the blind,
and turn your face to the Sun.
We are wholly, in fact, a miracle
waiting to realize ourselves.

Idealization is a process of projection that is rampant in our culture. It is a way of seeing that passes reality through a filter and embellishes it. The list of things that can be idealized is practically endless--other people, objects, situations, possibilities. Almost all humans are caught in idealization from time to time. It is usually invisible to us, because we believe that we are perceiving unvarnished reality. Psychology doesn't talk much about the normal process of idealization. It only enters psychological discourse when it becomes pathologically inflated. However, it has consequences in our lives, even at the normal levels. Those consequences can range from being perfectly harmless to being intensely destructive. The basic definition to keep in mind is a projection that distorts reality by leaving out the negative parts.

In the idealized projection, the subject is perceived as excessively beautiful or excessively perfect or excessively excellent. An idealization pushes the subject up into the spiritual realm ever so slightly and slightly spiritualizes it, so that it is more perfect, more beautiful and more excellent than it actually is.

Idealization is one of the fundamental processes in the human mind. The reason that we don't notice it is that it's folded seamlessly into our perceptions. It appears to be the actual way things are. It doesn't occur to us to question our perceptions. It just happens and we don't question it. It seems, when we are caught in an idealization, that we are perceiving reality, when in fact we are caught in a fantasy.

Let's take an example, say President Obama. There is an objective reality that is President Obama. He is a human who, like all of us, has flaws and can sometimes make mistakes, even bad mistakes. There is an idealized perception of Obama that sees him as a giant historical figure, the equal of Washington, Jefferson and Franklin (also idealizations). In this idealized perception, Obama is credited with having impeccable and unimpeachable judgment, flawless standards, and is in every way more excellent, more powerful, and more perfect than the reality of the man as he actually is. Notice that in the idealization the negatives (or possible negatives) have dropped off the screen, and we are left with a fantasy of excessive positivity.

You can see idealization at work most often in relationships, particularly romantic relationships. In fact, idealization appears to be a component in almost all romantic relationships. If we think back in our own experience, to the time when we first encountered someone who became very important romantically in our life, they were bathed in a certain kind of halo, a certain light. They became bigger than life. They became more perfect than they actually were, more satisfying than they actually were. In our perception of them, a gap formed between the reality of the person and the image that we carried in our mind of the person. That gap was a gap in perceiving reality. In this state, we no longer perceive reality. We perceive our idealized version of reality, and that gap in perception can be dangerous to our health.

Idealization is a component in the way that romance is understood in the Western mind. From the time of the Troubadours, when the concept of Western romantic love was formed, idealization has been accepted as a part of romantic love. The trouble is, because the idealized projection is not real, it cannot be sustained. Reality is not that perfect. As reality continues to unfold itself, as it grows up through the cracks, the fantasy of the idealization eventually cracks. It was never real. It was a projection, a fantasy, a delusion. It was a departure from reality from the beginning.

The test of a long, sustained relationship, either a marriage, friendship, or other relationship, is whether it can survive the period after the destruction of the idealizations. It is a given that, eventually, the idealizations will be destroyed. Anybody who has ever been married will agree. It is not possible to live with another person in a state of uninterrupted bliss forever. When an idealization emerges in our consciousness, when we project onto a subject more excellence than it actually possesses, the shadow side of the reality vanishes off the screen, leaving only the positive qualities, the ideal images in our head, to focus on. The shadow side of reality, however, still exists and is still there, and will eventually raise its head.

Idealizations are intimately related to hope. They are usually generated by the desire to find what we've been searching for, what we have been needing and yearning for in our life. When we perceive the subject in the world, it seems that we have found what we've been looking for. Because the longing already exists in our minds, we're very susceptible to idealization. It comes easily and invisibly. It feels like gratification and fulfillment. The way that hope differs from idealization is that, with hope, we can remain in touch with reality. We can remain firmly grounded, seeing all aspects of the subject, seeing the situation in all of its complexity, and still hope. With an idealization, we lose sight of reality. We become blind to reality. That is the important distinction between hope and idealization.

Idealizations usually have an element of future-orientation. They usually are accompanied by visions that the subject is going to play a wonderful part in our life in the future. We commence overstating the case, losing touch with reality in the process. Reality is always mixed. It always contains a shadow side and negative possibilities as well as a positive side. With idealization, the possible negative factors disappear. They vanish because we are no longer in touch with reality. We are in touch only with the positive images of our idealization. For us, and for the moment, the negative factors no longer exist. We focus intently and exclusively on the positive parts of the idealization.

In a very real sense, in the grip of an idealization we become blind. We become blind to the negatives and possible negatives in the subject--the person, the situation, the object, or the unfolding development. Idealization is a projection that propels us into fantasy or delusion. We can no longer see what's really out there in the world. Instead, we see our idealization, which does not truly exist. It exists only in our mind.

At this point, we have lost contact with reality. It has vanished, to be replaced by an unreal vision. For this reason, idealization can be very dangerous. If we have lost touch with reality, we are left helpless to make good decisions, to assess what needs to be done, and to deal effectively with the situation. We cannot effectively plan. We cannot effectively deal with life. We are left disarmed and vulnerable. We are no longer grounded, and we cannot see clearly. Our vulnerability is heightened by the fact that all this is invisible to us. Unless we have become aware of the danger of idealizations, we are prey to them and their consequences. Reality vanishes and we don't even realize it. In the grip of that loss of reality, we can make mistakes that alter the course of our lives.

When reality eventually breaks through the delusion, we experience the "cracking of the idealization." The emptiness and falseness of the idealization appear. At this point, when the idealization is challenged by emerging reality, we will often go to great lengths to try to keep the idealization viable. We will do contortions in our consciousness to keep it in place, because we are invested in it, depending on it.

In general, however, the cracking cannot be evaded. It continues. At this point, we usually realize that we have been caught in a delusion, that it was not real, that we have misperceived the subject, and that we have to give it up and accept the reality. The process of the cracking of an idealization is generally very painful. It is painful because we're so heavily invested in it. We want our lives to be just the way we pictured them with the idealization in place. We realize that it's not going to be that way. We realize that the idealization was false to begin with. Here, a sense of shame may arise, shame at having misperceived so thoroughly. When we finally see that our perceptions were not in accord with reality, it becomes clear to us that we perceived wrongly.

We may feel ashamed that we were so off base. The shame of having been lost in delusion makes it even harder to deal with the cracking of the idealization. That becomes part of the pain, the sense of shame at having allowed ourselves to see something that wasn't really there, that was never there. This raises the possibility that we can't trust our perceptions. It's quite a loaded issue to ask ourselves if we perceive reality fully or selectively.

Gripped by an idealization, we distort the world. We are separated from reality. We temporarily lose our clarity and ability to perceive reality as it actually is. When it cracks, people often shift to demonization. They go from considering the subject ideal and perfect to considering it demonic and disappointing on every count. They go to the opposite pole, because of the disappointment that the idealization was not true, the disappointment that their life is not going to be as they thought, and the disappointment in themselves for having been so mistaken. Also, under the influence of the idealization, we may have made mistakes that are very difficult to undo, such as marrying the wrong person. If we shift to the pole of demonization, we will not be able to see one good thing about the subject. It will seem totally wrong, totally deficient. This can be a delusion that is as divorced from reality as the original idealization. We have, at this point, shifted from a delusion at one pole to a delusion at the other pole. This often happens when the idealization cracks.

The goal to pursue is accurate, balanced perception that takes everything into account. We need to perceive reality with clarity, as it actually exists, with both positives and negatives intact, in all its complexity. Reality always exists with both upsides and downsides, with both sunlight and shadows. To manage our lives effectively, we need to see as much of reality in its wholeness as we possibly can. That means to actively look for the shadow side as well as the positive. If we can be aware of the process of idealization, we can be watchful for it and wary of it. Perhaps we can learn to catch it as it is forming, and sidestep it. When we know that idealization creates a delusional state, then we can try to avoid it. If we know that objective reality exists outside the idealization, we can make a conscious effort to balance our perceptions and find the objective perspective. If we realize that we are beginning to get hooked into an idealization, we can search for the reality that counter-balances it. It is very difficult to catch our own idealizations as they are emerging, because they are folded seamlessly into our perceptions, but it can be learned.

Nothing about taking charge of our idealizations precludes hope. As human beings, we will always be hoping to improve our lives. Our goal is to perceive reality with clarity, in all of its fullness. We can do that without succumbing to the blindness associated with idealization.